All Men Have Secrets

All Men Have Secrets

Tom Gallagher
Michael Campbell
Murdo Gillies

First published in Great Britain in 1995 by
Virgin Books
an imprint of Virgin Publishing Ltd
332 Ladbroke Grove
London W10 5AH

Reprinted 1997

A catalogue record for this book is available from the British Library

ISBN 0 86369 874 3

Typeset by TW Typesetting, Plymouth, Devon
Printed and bound in Great Britain by
Cox & Wyman Ltd, Reading, Berkshire

Contents

Foreword by John Peel   ix
Introduction   xi
Acknowledgements   xv

Accept Yourself   1
Ask   3
Asleep   7
Back To The Old House   9
Barbarism Begins At Home   11
Bigmouth Strikes Again   14
The Boy With The Thorn In His Side   19
Cemetry Gates   23
Death At One's Elbow   28
Death Of A Disco Dancer   32
Frankly, Mr Shankly   34
Girlfriend In A Coma   36
Girl Afraid   42
Half A Person   44
Hand In Glove   48
The Hand That Rocks The Cradle   52
Handsome Devil   55
The Headmaster Ritual   57
Heaven Knows I'm Miserable Now   59
How Soon Is Now?   69
I Keep Mine Hidden   84

I Know It's Over 88
Is It Really So Strange? 95
I Want The One I Can't Have 97
I Won't Share You 99
Jeane 102
Last Night I Dreamt That Somebody Loved Me 105
London 111
Meat Is Murder 113
Miserable Lie 115
Money Changes Everything 117
Never Had No One Ever 119
Nowhere Fast 121
Paint A Vulgar Picture 123
Panic 125
Please Please Please Let Me Get What I Want 130
Pretty Girls Make Graves 134
The Queen Is Dead 137
Reel Around The Fountain 143
Rubber Ring 151
A Rush And A Push And The Land Is Ours 155
Rusholme Ruffians 157
Sheila Take A Bow 161
Shoplifters Of The World Unite 164
Some Girls Are Bigger Than Others 167
Still Ill 172
Stop Me If You Think You've Heard This One Before 177
Stretch Out And Wait 179
Suffer Little Children 181
Sweet And Tender Hooligan 185
That Joke Isn't Funny Anymore 187
There Is A Light That Never Goes Out 189
These Things Take Time 203
This Charming Man 205
This Night Has Opened My Eyes 215
Unhappy Birthday 218
Unloveable 220

Vicar In A Tutu   222
Well I Wonder   225
What Difference Does It Make?   230
What She Said   238
William, It Was Really Nothing   241
Wonderful Woman   243
Work Is A Four Letter Word   245
You've Got Everything Now   247
You Just Haven't Earned It Yet, Baby   249

Discography   251

Foreword by John Peel

I never saw Elvis live. I never saw The Velvet Underground either, with or without Nico. I never saw The Stooges, The New York Dolls, The Sex Pistols or The Clash. I also never saw The Smiths. I particularly regret never seeing The Smiths.

The truth is, it wasn't even my idea to book the band for that celebrated first Radio One session (18 May '83). Rough Trade had sent me a demo tape – I still have it somewhere – but I hadn't yet had a chance to snuggle down with it when John Walters, then the programme's producer, came into the office and announced that he had seen The Smiths the previous evening. Now Walters didn't see many bands (Stevie Wonder at the Royal Albert Hall or some withered trad jazzers at the 100 Club being his idea of a reasonable time) so I was impressed.

I was even more impressed when Walters said something along the lines of 'We must book them for a session' and reached for the phone. This was unprecedented stuff. Mind you, Walters was absolutely right. Even now I still use The Smiths as an example – perhaps *the* example – of a band that arrived out of the blue without any apparent influences. You could listen to the demo tape, to that first Radio One session, to the subsequent records, and you couldn't tell what music Morrissey, Marr, Rourke and Joyce had hidden under their beds.

I've never met Marr, Rourke or Joyce but I did meet that Morrissey a couple of times. We did *Round Table* together. I don't remember any of the records played, although I bet there are Smiths/Morrissey fanatics who could tell me every track featured and every golden word the master uttered. His words were pretty golden too, so much so that I suspect he had honed one or two elegant phrases during the afternoon and simply applied them to whatever new release he was called upon to assess. The fact that Morrissey rejoiced so much in the use of language even in this context delighted me.

The second time our paths crossed was a chance meeting in those motorway services south of Newcastle-upon-Tyne. Sheila and I had just sat down to a delicious country bap or some such nonsense, when Morrissey appeared at our table. 'These are my favourite motorway services,' he announced. What sort of a man has a favourite motorway service area?

Later, as we headed home, Steve Wright was going on about what miserabilists The Smiths were. This staple of the afternoon programme never failed to enrage me. The best Smiths records often made me laugh out loud. They could be waspish, sardonic, even sentimental, but at their best they were the best. Which is probably why so many new bands trawling the past for inspiration stop off for a while with the second best band Manchester ever produced.

March 1995

Introduction

As we sit down to write, February 1995 draws to a close and with it, the eighteen dates of Morrissey's current 'Boxers' tour wend their way inexorably towards London and the Theatre Royal. In truth, the marvellous (if mistimed) distraction that has been the tour has had little direct bearing on the book's satisfactory completion, save, that is, for the opportunity it afforded to meet in person many of those whose names and hands have become so very familiar over the last ten months. It is intended as no slight whatsoever to the great man when we say that three of us, at least, regarded his appearance on stage as merely part of the evening's allure. If those we've been lucky enough to bump into at venues have been left with an impression only half as favourable as that which, invariably, they *made*, then we shall reflect contentedly upon having cut a mighty impressive gib.

It is, we reckon, well worthy of mention that one of the major talking points of the 'Boxers' tour so far has been the long awaited revival of the old Smiths favourite, 'Shoplifters Of The World Unite'. How the years rolled away. To paraphrase the song, if High Street kleptomaniacs *do* consider six months a long time, we can respond with confidence that the ten months over which *All Men Have Secrets* has been compiled has seemed a very *short* time. And while we're about it, would an order for two camcorders and a fridge-freezer be out of the question? No? Nice one . . .

All Men Have Secrets

A very short time in several respects. First, for those of us in whom the work ethic runs a poor second to the *mañana* instinct, a thousand years would seem a short time when there's a job to be done with a deadline imposed. There's a law which describes this, and it has nothing whatsoever to do with love and poverty – just simple fecklessness. Second, the sense of the surreal which bubbled to a head one summer lunchtime in Ladbroke Grove has never truly dissipated. Put simply, we can't believe we're doing this, and never quite have. When the germ of an idea which started life as little more than an antidote to boredom blossoms so spectacularly it can be difficult to grasp. What we've lacked in cognition, however, has been amply compensated for by an excitement which can best be described as childlike: the thrill heightened by our awareness of just how infrequently such dreams are realised. After all, those many, many thousands who switch off *Noel's House Party* on a Saturday evening to go and buy a lottery ticket can be said to be participating as an antidote to boredom. But few of them win. We did, and we've loved every minute. Time has flown because, third, we've been having an awful lot of fun. Every aspect of the project has been a joy and very little has felt like 'work' in the conventional sense of the word. Enormous has been the fun we've had placing, then spotting, the advertisements and replying to the ensuing deluge of letters. Waiting, excited and expectant, for Keith the postman to arrive never *did* lose its 'Christmas morning' appeal and the pleasure we've derived from reading a steady succession of fanzines owed little to the fact that many, if not most, were sent free of charge. The Smiths/Morrissey nights in Glasgow and Manchester and London always did seem an hour too short. Those many floors on which we've slept were curiously comfortable and (for two of us, at any rate) dawn's hangovers uncommonly forgiving. We've relished the opportunity to rattle on proudly and at length to anyone within earshot – most of whom appeared genuinely delighted to share the tiny measure of celebrity which accrued. That generosity of spirit was, in itself, a delight. And yes, we even contrived to have fun during the eight-hour over-night bus journeys from Glasgow to London. For us, the train never *did* heave on to Euston; rather, the coach chugged on to Charnock Richard. You know that something fairly special is afoot when you're dancing and laughing and finally living in Charnock Richard at three in the morning.

And so to the product of our less-than-tortuous toils. Well, if there's more to life than books, then this one can justifiably claim to be a shining example of perfect reciprocity, for it offers nothing much more than life. Or lives, to be accurate. It is un-deniably short on opinion, and shorter still on analysis. Both, we feel, are oft apt to be futile and boring and in any event, a band as special as the one which forms the central theme of this book deserves better. You will, however, find stories; stories about songs and about people. Stories connected with the songs of The Smiths as told by the people who listened to them, rapt. Above all, and without exception, the stories you will read are true, for when all is said and done, those are the only kind of stories worth telling.

They are, by turns, moving, poignant, insightful, uplifting and amusing. On occasions, they defy belief. They share, however, one common factor in that without exception, they are REAL – all true, every last one. The writers whose contributions expose – in a unique and personal way – that portion of life which might be filed under 'harsh realities' are perhaps too numerous to men-tion personally. On the lighter side, Andrew of Liverpool lives in the memory as someone for whom taking 24 cans of beer to a party is considered a mere 'token gesture'. He was sixteen at the time . . . You're welcome round our place anytime, Andrew. As indeed is everyone whose name appears between the covers of *All Men Have Secrets*. Our debt of gratitude cannot possibly be repaid through the limiting medium of words on paper – regret-tably, and unlike Morrissey's, ours is not a pen charged with genius ink. So for now, thank you all will have to suffice.

Tom, Mike and Murdo

Acknowledgements

By its very nature, the names of the people to whom we owe most are to be found scattered throughout the book. But extra special thanks are due to the following contributors, whose boundless zest for the cause went far beyond the written word:

Melanie Newman
Angie J. Lewis
Libby
Jo Cooper

In grateful recognition of the following – many of whom are scarcely familiar with The Smiths – but whose practical assistance, advice and enthusiasm were no less valuable for that:

Brimichian Productions
Mums Campbell and Gallagher
Nuala Elder and family
Martin Farrell
Ken Garner
Ross and Mr Paul at Graven Images
Jeff McCall at No. 24
Gregg McLeod
Fraser Middleton
James Montgomery
Douglas Morwood

Orange Coast College, Costa Mesa, CA
Ms C. Park
Jenny Parkin
Dave Ross
Andy Stevens and flatmates
Bob Thompson
All at Killarney Lane and Colorado Place

And finally, our hats are tipped to that most curious of breeds –
the fanzine editor. If exposure was the lifeblood of the project,
then it was harnessed most effectively (and most cost-effectively!)
through the pages of those 'zines run by:

Hannah Bayman – *Miserable Lies*
Bruce Duff – *A Chance To Shine*
Phill Gatenby – *This Charming Fan*
Travis Gravell – *Wilde About Morrissey*
Tracey Holloway – *Jammy Stressford*
Julia Riley – *True to You*
Dave Tseng and Russ Seekatz – *Sing Your Life*

The man in the background was played by Euan L. Cameron.

All Men Have Secrets is dedicated to us all.

Accept Yourself

NAOMI KANEKO of Tokyo, Japan

This song reminds me of two years ago. Then I was seventeen years old, high school girl. I hated myself and school. Then, the school meant nothing to me, I had almost no friend and lessons were so useless. What I did is to keep silent and sit in the chair and I lost flesh greatly. Then I was 34 kg. It was obvious that I was sick but I didn't know what happening to me. Of course I couldn't go to school and went to hospital. The doctor said that if you didn't come to the hospital you would die. I thought where was my heart and body?

For a few months or more, I must struggle with myself to take my body back. But my body came back to me soon. Heart? Yeah, I got it in exchange of the fact. It is the fact that I am no more than myself. So I accepted myself then. So when you will accept yourself? Tell me when will you!

(Presented verbatim.)

ANGIE J. LEWIS of Huddersfield, Yorkshire

I laughed out loud when I first heard 'Accept Yourself' (which was back in 1988, at home in Huddersfield on my trusty walkman) because it rang so very true. The part that concerns 'drawing up a plan' was especially funny, because that's *exactly* what I did! Instead of going out to as many places as possible in order to find a boyfriend and 'conquer love', I was incredibly antisocial and instead decided to write a book (about The Smiths, funnily enough!) to bring some meaning into my miserable little existence. But, as is typically the case, my book didn't really get off the ground, and I've yet to make my debut. I wanted to produce a literary effort that had a bit more substance than the then previous effort by Mick Middles. It was to have been written from the point of view of a fan, and would have covered the entire career of The Smiths. Unfortunately, I lost heart when my attempts to get interviews with the band didn't go according to plan, and anyway, Johnny Rogan's beaten me to it now! The lyric that concerns being 'sick and dull and plain' I also identified strongly with, as I believed that I was bloody useless to everyone and everything. The last thing I wanted to do was to accept myself. Luckily, I've managed to come to terms with what I am since those days, when I was both virtually dead *and* so very easily led. Although I still get days when I feel dead awkward and unsightly, I can at least (sometimes) smile about it now . . .

Ask

ROB MARSHALL of Wood Green, London

'Writing frightening verse . . .' One dark afternoon, while awaiting the arrival of *Blockbusters* on television, I answered an advert
for penpals in *Smiths Indeed*. In truth, I loathe the word 'penpals',
but to be candid it seems as accurate as any to describe those most
curious of relationships. There ignited a relationship between the
postman and I which would last four years. Letters would arrive
almost weekly from all parts of Europe and beyond. It was enough
to make a young man weep – I simply didn't know there were so
many interesting people breathing. I was still a miserable bastard,
but felt altogether more comfortable wearing my cloak of gloom.

If some of the letters bore embarrassing epithets like 'Moz Is
God', these slight indiscretions could be overlooked while awaiting that one message which would leave me panting on the bathroom floor.

There is one unwritten, but faithfully adhered-to law in my
home town which decrees that sensitive males cannot and will
not be accepted. Those in breach risk being dragged off to the
town hall and forced to watch rugby league videos.

STIG HELLEREN of Stavanger, Norway

I have an annual ritual stretching back to New Year's Eve 1986,
which involves my putting on 'Ask' at exactly 11.59 p.m. and
thereby ending and beginning each year on the perfect note.

3

All Men Have Secrets

JOANNE MADDOX of Walney Island, Cumbria

One stifling day in Ibiza in 1989 I met a Belgian lass named Iris; we got talking and she asked me what kind of music I liked. When I said The Smiths she shrieked in disbelief. She was so impressed – I almost felt like a Smith myself! I was to learn that being a Smiths apostle in Belgium was almost unheard of, and that Iris was viewed as being rather odd for liking them. Thanks to our musical bond we're friends to this day and have spent our fair share of 'alcoholic afternoons' sitting in rooms drawing up plans. One such plan was to backpack around Europe in '91.

With our 'Grand Tour' barely more than halfway completed, we found ourselves exhausted, in dire need of a good shower and semi-insane through lack of music. Typically overcautious, we'd decided not to pack our walkmans for fear of them being nicked. Daft really.

The last vestiges of our sanity were to desert us, appropriately enough, in Vienna – the beautiful city of music. Trudging past the pavement cafés thronged with *cappuccino*-sipping tourists we began caterwauling 'Ask'. What a contrast we must have made to the classical buskers – and I'm sure Mozart turned in his grave. Oddly enough, exhaustion seemed no longer to matter and neither did the fact that we were horribly smelly. On THIS day, shyness wasn't going to stop us from doing ANYTHING!

ALEXANDRA HINCKS of Bath, Avon

A most wonderful, magical masterpiece of a song! So wonderful and so magical, in fact, that I can reveal its status as the main ingredient in a recipe I used to transform a 'rave' maniac into a Smiths fan. A miracle? Well perhaps ...

And so the story goes. My roommate was always insistent on polluting our cramped little pit with rave tracks mixed by naff people with even naffer names such as 'Eezygroove'. This, added to the psychedelic wall decoration, was beginning to cause me severe headaches. I grabbed a brief respite one bright evening in May. She arrived home late to find my music play-ing. Not being totally inconsiderate, she conceded that, on this one occasion, Eezygroove would have to wait his turn. 'Ask' came on. She listened, she liked, she requested a repeat play. 'The Smiths,' I replied in answer to her enquiry, and liking turned quickly to bewilderment. That which she previously dis-missed was soon to become her passion!

Would you believe that she's now trying to grow a quiff? I tried to do this once, but am now content to bear a passing re-semblance to the girl in the 'Everyday Is Like Sunday' video. I must say it's a vast improvement to wake up in the morning to a huge poster of Moz rather than a poster of a huge spliff.

ALBERTO FORNI of Milan, Italy

The Smiths have always been a 'cult' band in Italy.

As a matter of fact, at a certain point – thanks to such songs as 'Bigmouth Strikes Again' or 'Some Girls Are Bigger Than Others' frequently transmitted on the radio – The Smiths seemed very likely to make it with the big Italian audience but then they split up, as we know.

In 1985 I had the chance to see The Smiths play live in Rome, in the only Italian concert of their career. I used to love them very much and make my friends listen to them, yet I didn't have any kind of contact with other Italian fans.

After their splitting up I have often wondered how many people remember them as dearly as I do. At the beginning of 1992 I finally decided to answer that question and started pub-lishing a fanzine, even though I had no experience whatsoever.

ASK! was born. It was a fanzine for Smiths and Morrissey fans, and dedicated to those who wish impossible things. I wanted it to be an 'open' publication, also speaking about other bands, cinema and literature, but always referring to a certain kind of sensitivity.

I advertised in some musical magazines and waited.

I thought nobody would answer me – yes, The Smiths have been an important group, but in Italy ... and five years after their splitting up, not to mention the fact that Morrissey is quite unknown here and has never played live in Italy.

I still remember the emotion I felt when I got the first letter, followed by many more.

The final result was excellent, given that it was the first Italian fanzine about The Smiths; over 200 people wrote to me and in addition to that, I've made friends with some of them, and we still see each other.

In 1994 we attended the first convention of Italian fan clubs at Modena. We felt a bit out of place next to fan clubs such as Europe's, Marillion's and others arranged by record companies much more powerful than we were. Yet our stand was full of joyful people – many of them had travelled 500 kilometres just to meet likeminded souls!

Two months later, we organised the first Italian Smiths day in a country house on Morrissey's birthday – a weekend of quizzes, Smiths karaoke, live music and the showing of video tapes by our favourites. That was a wonderful experience leading to new friendships.

And on that same occasion, what about meeting Massimiliano? He brought a shred of the shirt worn by Morrissey during the famous concert in Rome.

After seven issues I decided to cease publication because the commitment was too hard to handle, and what's more, after doing what I wanted to do, I needed to move to something else.

Anyway, not everything's lost – an *ASK!* reader is publishing a new Italian fanzine dedicated to Morrissey. It's called *Speedway* and two issues are available already.

After all, the most important thing was to discover and get together all the people scattered throughout Italy who still remembered the emotion contained in that *Hatful of Hollow*.

Asleep

GRAHAM COLEMAN of Hampstead, London

Missing her like I never thought possible 3,000 miles away and going to work with my walkman on and tapes of The Smiths and Aretha Franklin and Prefab Sprout and just baffled at what had happened to me. How did it ever come to this? And always shattered and hungover and one day walking back in the early spring sunshine and this came on with its howling wastes and I felt like crying and ripping off my suit and what was I doing carrying this fucking briefcase – it really was a miserable lie and longing to hold her or just to see her one more time . . .

TON DE VRIES of Rotterdam, Holland

A friend of mine remained alone as people around him fell in love, married, had children, had affairs, divorced, fell out of love, remarried and began all over again. Family and friends were puzzled. Was he gay? Was something wrong with him? I'm sure the social pressure he felt must at times have been too much to bear. I was once having a drink with him, and played *Louder Than Bombs*. He listened to this song, read the lyrics and confided in me that he recognised only too well this longing for sleep and early death. I was amazed – he seemed such a cheerful guy. How wrong can one be about someone?

I don't see him much now, but he sent me a card not long ago. After all these years he's married with a lovely baby girl and lives in a neighbourhood where the most important thing is keeping your garden tidy. I guess he's found his peace at last. To me he is asleep right now, but everybody's got to live their lives, I suppose (and God knows . . .).

MARTIN COOPER of Glasgow, G2

A friend of mine recounted a great Smiths story. She was a fanatic, wearing her hair in a quiff and always sporting a Smiths T-shirt from what seemed to be an inexhaustible collection. The day after a gig, she was walking her dog along the windswept and nearly deserted seafront at Morecambe. In a shelter, usually the haunt of a gang of old dears, was huddled the band. She chatted eagerly to an amicable Johnny Marr who kept shifting uncomfortably as Morrissey was fast asleep and resting his head on Johnny's shoulder. A fabulous scene which never fails to pop into my head when I hear this song.

CHARLOTTE HALL of Leith, Edinburgh

My mum's name is Marg. One of her friends – Patrick – died during an epileptic fit. He was in his early thirties. I didn't realise that Marg even listened to the music I played, although I suppose she could hardly avoid it since I played it loud in the living-room. One day she told me that 'Asleep' really meant something to her because of Patrick. Despite the fact that I never really knew him, this song will always evoke that sharp sense of loss because Marg cried on hearing it.

Back To The Old House

KENT BURT of St John's, Newfoundland, Canada

I visit my home town once, maybe twice, a year. Nothing ever changes. I'm still filled with dread and boredom while there. It's like I've never been away; still thinking about the same old failures and all the people I liked who never knew it. This song is very real to me. I could have written it. There was even a person who cycled by . . .

MARTIN COOPER of Glasgow

She wasn't pretty; a fat face, short hair and big arse. All the other staff were *Baywatch* babes and bronzed bastards. They waited on and she was just the humble prep-chef. She didn't talk much, preferring instead to play tapes in the kitchen and keep herself to herself. 'Suedehead' came on. Yeah, she loved Morrissey and The Smiths, The Dead Kennedys and Pil. We rocked and rolled and lumbered our way round to her house in a huge seventies Oldsmobile. This house was a big ol' American house – straight from the movies. All grass verge, porch, rocking-chair and dog. Inside we were met by her even fatter mom, a multitude of pot Marys, Pope portraits and plastic crucifixes. Her bedroom must have been mom's idea of hell . . . !

All Men Have Secrets

ANDY PINCHEN of Bridgwater, Somerset

From 1980 to 1985 I attended Sydenham Comprehensive School in Somerset. There (as you do!), I fell in love for the first time with a girl in my class. Teenage crush maybe, but Wendy Grace simply took my young heart, although much of my love and most of my thoughts for her went unrequited and overlooked. But of course the story was an old one . . . I was just a little too shy and Wendy was, well, just Wendy. Schooldays have a nasty habit of finishing just a week too soon and before long we were going our separate ways with hardly so much as a 'goodbye'. 'Back To The Old House', with its weighty sense of regret, sums up that feeling of lost opportunity. 'And you never knew how much I really liked you/Because I never even told you, oh and I meant to.'

Barbarism Begins At Home

TON DE VRIES of Rotterdam

I was standing on a crowded train to Belgrado, then still part of Yugoslavia. *Meat is Murder* was playing on my walkman. A Serbian girl (who reminded me of Ingrid Bergman) asked if she might listen for a minute. She listened to 'Barbarism . . .' and it seemed as if she'd been struck by lightning. We had a conversation that was incredibly intimate for two people just meeting on a train. I saw her one time after that, in the famous Belgrado bar named '?'. Sadly, we didn't exchange addresses. On hearing this song I still see her 'Casablanca' face and wonder what has become of her during that tragic war in her country.

RUSS C. S. THOMAS of Ferndale, South Wales

'Barbarism . . .' remains my favourite track from *Meat is Murder*. I'd have killed my mother to see Pete Burns shaking his tambourine on stage with Morrissey to this. I associate it with schooldays and the sixth form common-room and the notorious Newport gig. Yes, *that* one at which Morrissey was dragged down and nearly lynched by a crowd of hostile Cardiff City supporters who had gathered near the front. For me, the excitement didn't quite end that night.

Next morning, a girl I knew was filing tapes below the

counter in Spillers, an independent music store in Cardiff. Hearing a polite cough, she looked up to be faced by a rather battered and bruised Morrissey. Managing to stay relatively calm, she bagged up the George Formby album he was buying, rang the till and promptly rang me up. There followed a frantic hunt round Cardiff, but he was nowhere to be seen. Another friend did report sighting Morrissey in Lears bookshop, but despite my best efforts, our paths were not fated to cross that day.

KATE HANLON of Dublin

Even as the youngest of five, the shameless acts of petulance which peppered my childhood were wholly inexcusable. I got away with murder, secure in the knowledge that, as Daddy's little princess, retribution would be slight. My four elder brothers (the only fraternity visible from space – they're huge!) were something envied deeply by other children, and to my mind, rightfully so.

All this was to change in 1986 when my smugness began to manifest itself slightly differently in modest helpings of rebellion. The adult pastimes deemed appropriate for my all-new reinvented persona were, variously, smoking, boys and The Smiths. The last two caused barely a ripple of disapproval; Mum and Dad effortlessly forgave my appalling taste in boys, and Morrissey's loud tones, if not exactly in the house top ten, were tolerated none the less. The smoking, however, was taboo. They detested smoking. With four fit lads as a testament to clean, healthy living, this was one boundary I was going to find hard to push back. Furtive, late-night cigarette butts were deposited in the window-box on my bedroom ledge. Mercilessly put upon, the flowers were dead by early May.

One morning we slept in – an innocuous enough event but one which triggered a chain of events which ended in dire consequence. Father ran me to school in the car, depositing me there before driving on to work. I waved him goodbye and promptly scuttled the 100 yards or so to a local newsagent – my regular, unquestioning supplier of smokers' requisites. But drive on to work he didn't. He must have reparked the car as I entered the shop. He must have locked the door as I drank in the sight of Morrissey writhing majestically over that morning's cover of the *NME*. He must have opened the shop door just as I nonchalantly requested 'the usual' ten Silk Cut and a box of matches . . .

Whipped to within an inch of my (tar-shortened) life and The Smiths on the headphones for days and weeks afterwards, barbarism might not have begun at home but it sure as hell finished there.

Bigmouth Strikes Again

HUGH RYCROFT of Oval, London

As a long-standing fan, my friend Jason thought it might be a good wheeze to slip a Smiths cover into his band's set at the school rock concert. This was of more than passing interest to me, since I was due to be sharing vocals on that particular number. It occurred to us that the wheeze might be better still were we to perform an as yet unreleased track with which the audience would be unfamiliar. No problem! A bootleg tape of the benefit gig The Smiths had played for Liverpool City Council furnished us with just such a song: 'Bigmouth Strikes Again'.

We listened intently, over and over again, trying desperately to discern the lyrics from this typically lo-fi bootleg. The great day arrived, and in our best Morrisseyesque voices we warbled, 'Sweetness, sweetness I was only joking when I said I'd like to smash a meat-hook in your face . . .' Well, it was almost right.

TOM HALL of Southgate, London

In my experience, 'Bigmouth . . .' is all too often used as bait to lure quiffed-up kids on to indie dancefloors. In truth, this is hardly surprising: the opening chords are so anthemic and defiant that they often make you explode with joy.

One bitter Tuesday evening in '92 my brother and I made a

14

rare visit to Camden Palace's notoriously awful indie club. Some band or other who we quite fancied were on. While shivering in the queue, four smiling blokes ran up to us shouting, 'The Smeeths, Morrizzee!' A bit confused, we nodded and confirmed that, yes, we were Smiths fans and at this they broke into even-more-delighted grins. 'Ow Soon Eez Now,' one said, apparently the leader. 'The Queen Is Dead,' I replied, to which a previously silent member of the group added, 'Ah, Veekar In A Tu-Tu!' This 'conversation' bubbled along in much the same vein for several minutes until the time came to bid farewell with a group hug.

Inside the club and glad to be out of the cold, we spotted the Swedes (for that is where they hailed from) trying vainly to chat up unimpressed girls wearing Ned's T-shirts. I can only surmise that the technique they'd tried on us did not hit the spot! As if on cue, 'Bigmouth . . .' struck up and our Anglo-Swedish alliance was cemented on the dancefloor during three minutes of frantic, manic Mozzing around.

HOWARD TINKER of Crewe, Cheshire

A *Top of the Pops* hell. A tawdry, tacky twilight world where Boys-In-Suits meet Girls-In-Perms. Here, 'neath the flashing strobes, did I first fall in love.

It's the annual college end-of-pier disco, Southport, June 1986. I'm sporting a black polo-neck and bright pink cardigan, but at seventeen can hardly be expected to know better. A friendly girl says I look 'trendy' but I suspect she's just being kind. Myself and Adam (colleague in teen angst) nervously nurture pints as we survey the heaving dancefloor. Everybody seems to be whooping it up except us. Adam suggests we go over and talk to two goth girls sitting in a corner, but I talk him out of it. Frankly, I'm drunk and want to go home. And then . . .

'It's The Smiths,' cries the DJ and something magical happens.

The dancefloor clears in seconds and the Proustian rush of singing, ringing acoustic guitars seems amplified. Then the drums
steam in and the song kicks into life.

'Sweetness, sweetness I was only joking when I said I'd like
to smash every tooth in your head . . .'

As the song sweeps across the empty floor I'm mesmerised.
It's like the moment in *The Wizard of Oz* when the world
changes from grey monochrome into dazzling technicolour. Life
can hinge on moments like these, and without even believing in
corners, I've just turned one.

It is the most amusing, exciting, passionate thing I've ever
heard. I sip my beer and contemplate; things feel different now.
Walking home alone through the cold, empty streets I hum
'Bigmouth . . .' all the way and wear a smile which couldn't be
surgically removed.

Next day, I stagger into town at the crack of noon and purchase *The Queen is Dead* from a plump lady with a moustache
in W. H. Smith. Back home, fumbling the stylus on to the
crackling black vinyl, I know something is about to happen.

MARY DAVIS of Margate, Kent

Shortly before leaving school, some friends and I formed a
band. At the time it was merely a scam to avoid geography
classes, but it developed into our mid-teen salvation. The head-
mistress, wishing to satisfy herself that we were spending the
time profitably, asked us to play at our final assembly.

We had a little set of four songs and 'Bigmouth . . .' was pencilled in as the big finish. As a gimmick to rival the Stonehenge
scene in *Spinal Tap*, we enveloped one of our posse in a sack
and tied it securely with ropes and a volleyball net. The idea
was that he should jump around in Houdini fashion while we
played.

We got underway and having executed the first three songs
pretty successfully, began to grow in confidence. Disaster

however, was lurking just around the corner. During 'Bigmouth . . .' our man in the sack fell over and, being quite unable to see or find his footing, began rolling manically around the stage. He knocked over our guitarist, destroyed much of the drum kit and finally plunged over the edge of the stage to the utter delight of the ruffian audience. This story and the song itself recalls a time when I was having fun without the complications which adulthood inevitably brought.

BRIAN MATTHEWS of Camberley, Surrey

I spent the latter part of my school career at a non-private boarding establishment – and no, it wasn't borstal. At places of this kind, the night staff generally conform to one of two types: the maternal kind or the army sergeant-major. You never were quite sure who would be doing the rounds on any given evening.

I spent many a midnight hour secretly listening to those sparkling Radio One sessions and longing to get caught – preferably by the sergeant-major. 'Bigmouth . . .' reminds me of this period. Sadly, I never did get caught, my bid for glory usually being pre-empted by some big-mouthed creep.

MELINDA HSU of Fresno, California, USA

Ever been to Fresno? No? Fresno is famous for three things – heat, homicide and raisins. I hate all three. My feelings about Fresno are relevant to, and indeed largely responsible for, my feelings about The Smiths. While Fresno, to the untrained eye, is a large metropolitan city within a state known for its large, metropolitan cities, I found it unbearbly dull and stifling. It was especially hard being different, alone and somewhat 'aware', if you know what I mean. The radio stations offered nothing more uplifting than the American Top Ten and country music to appease the valley girls.

I first heard The Smiths when a cousin of mine came over from Los Angeles, bringing with him *The Queen is Dead*. It was Christmas '86 and we were vacationing at Lake Tahoe where an old school friend from Reno, Nevada, also came to stay. He was really taken with the lyrics to 'Bigmouth . . .', and dug the line, 'Sweetness, sweetness I was only joking when I said I'd like to smash every tooth in your head.' If this gave me slight cause for concern about my friend, I reminded myself that he was an unusually intelligent and sensitive guy. Yet those types often harbour a wicked sense of the perverse. Step forward, Morrissey!

GEMMA MALTBY of Brentwood, Essex

It was Valentine's Day and I was having a terrible time. I was at a nightclub with all of my friends and everything seemed to be going wrong. To gain admission to the club I had to kiss an awful boy to pretend we were going out together, as entry was for couples only. I was so embarrassed I wanted to leave there and then but having come so far I decided to stay. It was a huge mistake. Once inside, I felt very anti-social, ugly and horrible and I wished I hadn't bothered going. Then this boy who I had deeply fallen for was seen getting it together with some bitchy girl who I hated, so I was simply heartbroken. Just about to launch into a sulky miserable mood, imagine my relief on hearing the beginning of 'Bigmouth Strikes Again'. I jumped on the dancefloor and for a couple of minutes I forgot about everything and let myself go. Now whenever I hear that song I'm reminded of the intensity of that crush and how upset it made me, but most of all how good it was to hear The Smiths when I really needed them.

The Boy With The Thorn In His Side

STIG HELLEREN of Stavanger, Norway

I well remember this track being played on Norwegian national radio in October '85. The ineptitude of their DJs had, for years, been a source of amusement to me but on this occasion, I was incensed when the presenter introduced the song with the immortal words, 'Here's the new single from Liverpudlian duo The Smiths, currently huge in Britain.'

TOM GALLAGHER of Giffnock, Glasgow

In the late summer of 1985, I started my very first full-time job as a standbuilder at the now-defunct Anderston Exhibition Centre in Glasgow. It was employment for which I was spectacularly ill-suited, but with good pay and limitless overtime I was soon to become a very well-heeled eighteen year old. Much of the time was spent building and dismantling modest exhibitions at the Glasgow premises. We did, however, travel from time to time, setting up shows in venues throughout Scotland – Edinburgh, Stirling, Perth, Greenock and so on.

My arrival at Anderston coincided with the run up to the biggest annual event on the calendar – a massive trade fair at the five-star Coylumbridge Hotel near Aviemore. (It may have been called The Royal Scottish something-or-other, but I really can't recall.) This meant being up in the Highlands for nearly a fortnight, with big money to be made and a spending allowance and B&B accommodation and so forth. As October approached and anticipation built among my colleagues, I became familiar with the legends of years past: rampant sexual adventure with the businesswomen who would be in residence (and, I was assured 'on heat') that fortnight. If this *did* sound vaguely attractive, I was realistic enough to know that these glossy-lipped, high-heeled movers and shakers would be unlikely to look favourably upon a plump, eighteen-year-old virgin complete with second-hand wardrobe and mutant quiff.

I hated it – every miserable minute of it. I loathed the work. I dreaded the blinding, spirit-sapping hangovers which followed the monster drinking binges for which I was ill-prepared. Most of these took place in The Woodshed, a violent, dingy, small-town dive populated with screwball locals who might have stepped straight from the set of *Deliverance*. The business-women, meantime, guzzled vodkatinis amid the cheeseplants of the discreetly-lit hotel bars . . .

My sole comfort that fortnight was one Graeme Davidson, a student working the holiday with whom I got along well and who shared much of my distaste for the whole, sleazy set-up. That, and this song, which was newly released and played constantly by us on the jukebox at The Woodshed. 'The Boy With The Thorn . . .' is very possibly my favourite Smiths single, but I still cannot hear it without shuddering . . .

MARCO BILYK of Basingstoke, Hampshire

Home alone in Rome (well, staying with family) in the summer of 1986. I would get up around noon in a deserted apartment and watch TV while getting ready to go out. In between videos by Dire Straits and Prince, 'The Boy With The Thorn In His Side' would appear on the music channels at regular intervals. As such it became the first Smiths song I could recite word perfect and I remember on more than one occasion swaying about the apartment doing my Morrissey impersonation as it played, one hand on hip, struggling with the harmonies. Welcome respite from the incessant Eurobeat.

SARAH AXSON of Gerrards Cross, Buckinghamshire

I was punched in the face while listening to *The Queen is Dead* on a bus. Clearly, the person who dealt the blow was pissed off with my friend and I proudly rendering 'The Boy With The Thorn . . .' at full volume. Perhaps she was in love with Morrissey's sweet tones and didn't much approve of the cover. Perhaps she didn't care for The Smiths at all, or perhaps she was just aggressive.

STEVE COLLINS of Cheltenham, Gloucestershire

In 1985, I finally threw off the critical constraints of friends and family and took the fashion plunge.

The beginning of a new school year had heralded a fresh crop of newly clothes-conscious sixteen year olds desperate to carve their sartorial identity on an institution notoriously suspicious of anything more adventurous than blazer and tie.

Until then, I had been a mere fashion dilettante – content to invert my school tie in order that only the slim portion was on view. Neckwise, the objective was to achieve a knot so tiny in size that it might resemble a fly on the anchor of the *QE2*, and with this, for the time being, I was perfectly content.

My sights and ambitions were to be raised irrevocably upon purchasing a *Smash Hits* or *No. 1* or some such teen-mag. Scanning page upon page of tittle-tattle, I chanced upon a picture of The Smiths accompanying either the lyrics to, or short article on 'The Boy With The Thorn In His Side'. The whole idea of the song appealed to me greatly, but not nearly so greatly as two other things which sprang immediately from the photograph: Andy Rourke's brown suede slip-ons! I *had* to have a pair and, with money yet left over from a conveniently timed birthday, boasted the wherewithal to invest in one.

Deed done, I arrived at school the following Monday resplendent in all my Smithsular glory. A set of cheap wooden beads nestled between a hairless chest and the bri-nylon shirt for which a replacement had yet to be acquired. Hair slightly quiffed and rock solid, the shoes did seem to have lost something in transition from Andy's feet to my own size nines! Not to worry – display them to best effect I was determined to do, and this was achieved by turning up my school trousers some four inches or so.

Perhaps a third of a foot was a tad overzealous, for instead of garnering the desired compliments in the shoe department, I quickly became the bemused butt of a barrage of 'Has your budgie died?' jokes. The mockery only stiffened my resolve to be different. In a strange way, I even became quite attached to my newfound nickname. Schoolmasters, despite publicly pillorying me for it, even adopted it and to many I remain 'Budgie' even now. 'Budgie' Collins – the boy with the thorn in his side and the suede on his feet.

Cemetry Gates

Ms KAZUMI KOMURA of Yokohama, Japan

Some dreadly sunny days ago, there was a school. It was called Johnny Marr High School. There were three students and one headmaster. The students were called Steven, Andy and Mike and the headmaster's name was Johnny. They studied very high-technical guitar from headmaster, but only on dreadly sunny days.

However, one dreadly sunny day the headmaster lost his temper because all his school students did not come to play guitar well although he tried so hard to teach them.

I guess that's why The Smiths reached to end. Oh, this school's name wasn't Johnny Marr High School after all, but The Brixton Academy.

(Presented verbatim.)

JOANNE MADDOX of Walney Island, Cumbria

Paris – October '92. The obligatory visit to EuroDisney followed hard on the heels of food poisoning, so I needed to cheer myself up. Having 'done' most of the city before, I dragged a reluctant friend along to some famous cemetery gates on a not-so-sunny day. Stepping through those gates was like entering a different world; I remember it so vividly.

This special place seemed cloaked in an eerie atmosphere which was both scary and strangely fascinating. Despite being close to my friend I felt alone and isolated. As we trekked onwards through the monumental site it was impossible to ignore the 'Jim this way' graffiti. A gusting wind breathed life into the storm-damaged trees which hung low and precariously over desecrated graves. Startled cats appeared as if from nowhere before vanishing once more between the tombs and trees. After walking for over an hour and suffering the moans of my unwilling companion I finally came upon the object of my search: Oscar Wilde. Collapsing beside his stone I took time to reflect; no longer feeling uneasy and threatened I took time to smile. The monument betrayed signs of recent cleaning and stood out from its dull and decaying neighbours like a polished shell on a polluted beach. Very little graffiti had survived the scrub-up save for one large 'Morrissey' scrawled above the legend. A myriad of dead and dying flowers lay scattered on its ledges, merely highlighting one single stem of beautiful white gladioli. Venturing round the back I was to discover 'Passions just like mine' daubed in Morrissey's honour, as well as addresses and even photographs jammed into nooks and crannies.

My experience had been a most moving one – a curiously affecting mixture of disquiet and awe. It will, I know, remain vivid forever.

JONATHAN HASSALL of Chadderton, Lancashire
(Cemetry Gates/I Know It's Over)

Probably through morbidity more than any other factor, these two tunes remain my fondest.

I was, for a number of years, an altar boy at the local Catholic church which adjoined our school. By far the biggest perk of the job was being able to dodge morning lessons once or twice (but never thrice!) weekly. This peculiar 'treat' came about on the occasions of requiem masses being held. More often than not, these would involve attending the burial or cremation, thus further extending my absence from the classroom.

Ceremonial protocol dictated that I would travel ahead in the hearse, meaning that I would almost always arrive in good time. So what would I do? Read the gravestones, of course – in accordance (or compliance or coincidence?) with the lyrics of 'Cemetry Gates'.

Then, as the interment began, a different lyric would howl through my mind: 'Oh Mother, I can feel the soil falling over my head.'

Sitting in a religious class some hours later, I'd nurse proudly the fiver I'd been 'slipped' by the undertaker and reflect contentedly on the equitable world in which I lived . . . then.

SANDRA McMAHON of Wythenshawe, Manchester

This song immediately had the personal touch for me since the school I attended (1976–81) was situated at the bottom of Nell Lane and if we were early we would walk through the cemetery idly reading the gravestones. I even had my obligatory piece of literature under the arm – *Henry IV Part One*, if memory serves. I like to think that this was the same period that Morrissey spent pondering in similar vein.

PETE of Wylde Green, Warwickshire

I suppose that many people's recollections will centre around Père Lachaise for obvious reasons, but mine concern a very different place.

During the cold winter months of '89, I was lucky enough to find myself in Thailand for a couple of weeks. As usual, my Smiths collection had been faithfully packed along with the guide books and insect cream. My story begins at dawn one morning prior to embarking on the arduous coach excursion which would take us up-country to visit the River Kwai Bridge.

All Men Have Secrets

By mid-morning the sun was burning and a lunch stop in the jungle did nothing to lesson the irony of seeing posses of Japanese tourists snapping away as if for their very lives. As the ancient bus grunted onward, I drifted in and out of a bizarre sequence of dreams punctuated by snatches of *The Queen is Dead*. We finally reached the bridge location with the sun now directly overhead and the temperature somewhere around 120 degrees. It came as a blessed relief to enter the cool River Museum with its impressive and affecting collection of war memorabilia – paintings, diaries, reconstructed living quarters and much else. There followed a boat trip along the river and underneath the bridge itself before we alighted alongside one of the many cemeteries kept by the Thai people in honour of those who died.

My mental picture of the song's cemetery was, until then, one of lush undergrowth, damp, moss and hanging mist: 'A dreaded sunny day.' But as I surveyed this spartan, sun-baked and immaculately maintained site, it occurred to me that here lay a collection of people who had real cause to wake up trembling with fear on 'dreaded sunny days'.

LAURENCE HUGHES of Tufnell Park, London

In 1992 I was in the newly renamed St Petersburg, Russia, for a music festival. It was incredibly hot summer weather, I remember, and I was staying with a Russian friend, Kirhill, in a flat in one of those huge apartment blocks that stand in serried ranks in the suburbs of the city. Russia can be a terribly exhausting place to be in, and one afternoon I decided to stay in and have a rest from rushing around in the sun. On my own, I picked up a book of English verse published for use in Russian schools, and started to read. It had all the usual stuff – Shakespeare, Donne, Wordsworth, Keats and Yeats. It was bright sunshine outside, but the flat was very dark, and as I read I started feeling the most intense homesickness I've ever known.

It was like a physical illness hitting me, almost. The familiar words had made me suddenly and acutely aware of the strangeness and unfamiliarity of everything surrounding me. Russia feels so vast – all those windswept steppes and mountains and icy wastes going on for ever and ever; and it can be a bleak place, even when the sun shines. I felt so depressed I hardly knew what to do. But in the flat was a copy of *The Queen is Dead* belonging to Kirhill (I'd alerted him to The Smiths when he'd visited London a year or two before). I put it on the massive radiogram, stuck the headphones on my head, and wallowed. It was the perfect remedy, totally burying myself like that in glorious nostalgia. I'd never felt so strongly before the quintessential *Britishness* of The Smiths (and this is nothing to do with mindless nationalism). 'First known when lost' is how some poet or other expressed that sense of recognition. The evocation of gritty Northern streets, desolate but somehow romantic urban landscapes out of L. S. Lowry – it was all just overwhelming. When it came to 'Cemetry Gates' – adolescent angst among the gravestones – I literally had tears in my eyes. But I felt a lot better afterwards.

To paraphrase Noël Coward: 'Funny how potent pop music can be!'

Death At One's Elbow

CHERYL KRUNKROSKI of Franklin Park, New Jersey, USA

My younger brother Glenn died in a tragic accident. Two years later, I was lying alone in bed one night, fondly recalling our youth. I said to myself, 'OK, let's change the subject and listen to some tunes on the college station.' My blurry eyes were still shedding big tears when I heard a song bearing his name and intoning, 'Goodbye, my love – goodbye.' Coincidence or what? Despite my extremely stuffy head, I purchased *Strangeways* . . . the very next morning, its release day. My first Smiths album.

PETE of Wylde Green, Warwickshire

Back in '82, my grandparents moved from Leicester to be nearer my family. Little did I know then that my gran was suffering from cancer and had already undergone surgery to remove a growth. Watching them age together over the next few years, I had no inkling of the pain and emotional suffering they were both enduring, so wrapped up was I in my own adolescent capers.

In summer '85, my gran was still very ill despite the chemotherapy being insisted upon by my grandfather who could not bear the thought of losing her. One afternoon we were sitting in the garden making smalltalk when she turned to me and said,

'Pete, you know I'm going to die, don't you?' I did know by then, but brushed the subject aside with a flippant, 'No way, Gran – you've got plenty of years to come.'

She died that September, and this song will forever recall those mixed emotions of relief and anguish, as well as that throwaway comment intended only to comfort my gran.

ELIZABETH ROBINSON of Liverpool

My parents divorced in 1980 and as a result I became what one could reasonably term a 'handful'. A host of new 'uncles' floated in and out of my early teenage years with metronomic precision. Mum would meet a new bloke, be instantly smitten and invariably have shed his predecessor by the end of the following week. At least, that's all I could see. How she must have wished that myself and my younger sister Emma had opted for a life with Dad in Stockport. At the time I didn't notice how much of a weight around her neck we really were. She did her best to ensure we didn't become latchkey kids but rather than show some respect for her valiant efforts, all she got from me were barbed comments about how fat, ugly, bald or smelly her latest beau was. I blamed her lack of attention on whoever she chose to go out with. The reality was that she worked in a school during the day as a dinner lady and at night held down the unenviable position of taking cash at the door of a local nightclub. Exhausted and doubtless a little flattered by the male attention this post brought, she was often accompanied when returning home in the early hours. We could tell if she was interested in him if she popped her head round the bedroom door to inform us that 'our packed lunches were ready and that Uncle Tony or Bob or Jim had left a special treat (usually a Mars bar or something grabbed from a late-night garage) for us and wasn't he a lovely considerate man?'

For years I would hear none of it. None of those prospective stepfathers were up to scratch. That was until the appearance of Ian. He was different. He laughed heartily at the idea of being 'Uncle Ian'. He was good-looking and trendy and most importantly his musical tastes and mine were very definitely cut from the same aural cloth. We would spend hours slagging off each other's 'periphery bands' as he called them. I'd make a comment about the Bunnymen and he'd have a go about James. Quid pro quo and all that. Things were different though when it came to The Smiths. Words like 'genius', 'splendour', 'enlightening' and 'majesty' were bandied about on almost a daily basis.

I remember around this time that Emma suddenly suffered a short bout of eczema. Eczema is a skin condition which, the doctors informed us, can be brought on by stress. Mum immediately blamed the now almost forgotten divorce and resolved to find a cure.

About three weeks later Ian popped round to our house unexpectedly one Saturday morning. He had been doing his usual routine of going for a couple of pints before going to see Everton and had got chatting to a bloke in a pub who insisted that goat's milk was a surefire remedy for Emma's problem. He had wasted no time in borrowing his mate's car and insisted that we take a drive down to his cousin's farm in Wales to secure the milk which would promote Emma's return to health.

I remember belting down the motorway with Ian and Emma at 80mph with the windows down and *Strangeways . . .* playing. I began to imagine we were in some dangerous car chase or playing the lead in a film where the heroes only have a matter of minutes to save the planet. *Strangeways . . .* became the soundtrack of the film and 'Death At One's Elbow' (because of its obvious connotations) the track I mentally pencilled in for a single release to promote it. It would have made a good title for a film, don't you think?

To cut a long story short, we got the milk, named the goat Morrissey and saved the princess. About three months later, Ian's cousin Barry called us to see if we'd had any luck with the potion. I told him we had and that we'd been buying it locally ever since.

'You should come back down and get some more of Morrissey's own,' he laughed. 'Only he's in bed with the missus right now!' He went on to explain that the goats often roved about the house and occasionally ended up in their bed of all places. I sometimes wonder if Talbot Rothwell ever lived in Wales!

Death Of A Disco Dancer

GARETH HOPKINS of Cardiff, South Glamorgan

Aberystwyth: university town, Welsh Nationalist stronghold and home to countless shops peddling mystic crystals and love beads. And . . . no disco! The year was 1988 and the summer hot. Personal stereo on, exams and routine had been forgotten. Whatever drink was being cheaply promoted along the seafront in a glass by my side, the pastime of watching the setting sun blend to an orangey syrup with the sea had become an institution.

With the voice of Morrissey and Marr's guitar, *that* song, 'Death Of A Disco Dancer', slowly trickled into my head and the mood was set for contemplation. Although the song is not about leaving a specific person or place, it did seem to encapsulate that period of my life. Thinking long and hard about where I was at . . . Perhaps Terry Pratchett got it right with *Disc World* after all.

JENNIFER BRUNDAGE of San Jose, California, USA

My first term at college, playing *Strangeways* . . . night after night in the dorm. This song connects with a nervous night before a date with someone I'd met in a bookstore line – we'd got talking thanks to a Smiths T-shirt! So there I was, trying on lots of different clothes, thinking about the person and listening to '. . . Disco Dancer' at full blast. Even without this specific instance, the song always seemed to be around in a strangely comforting way. Very nice, very nice, very nice . . .

JAMES HOLLAND of Leeds, West Yorkshire

My brother and I were never close and rarely got on; a bit difficult considering we had to share a room. I was a year younger, much quieter than him, and he could never understand that I actually *wanted* to stay in at night listening to Andy Kershaw. He was much more of an extrovert and always out somewhere; a real disco kid with terrible dress sense. He hated The Smiths so I played them continually. As far as I was concerned, he was the most shallow person I knew, and I used to taunt him with this record when he was getting ready to go out. He left home when he was seventeen; no wonder really.

Frankly, Mr Shankly

IAN GOLDSACK of Maltby, South Yorkshire

A sarcastic, vitriolic cartoon of a song. Might we all yearn occasionally to become Mr Shankly and enjoy his undoubted power and influence? No, on second thoughts . . . It certainly wasn't the case when I broke loose in the cookery class one afternoon and proclaimed to the astonishment of all (particularly the deputy head who was taking the class), 'Frankly, Miss Brockwell, I care little for the cultivation of crumbs and carrots, nor for the baking of buns.' I earned a week's detention for my trouble, which was infinitely more agreeable than learning how to arrange a salad.

KEITH WRIGHT of County Armagh, Northern Ireland

The connections of this song are fairly obvious – I'm sure many a boss has shrivelled a little under its vitriolic onslaught! Liverpool fans such as myself might also recall for a moment a great man whom nobody, especially in Lanarkshire or on Merseyside, ever considered a 'flatulent pain in the arse'. Anything but . . .

BERNARD DOWNES of Norwich, Norfolk

For some reason, around the time of my seventeenth birthday, I found myself wallowing in a strange nostalgia, for a world I

34

never knew. I wanted it to be 1966, not 1986. I wore an old, battered top hat, thin winklepicker boots, striped, hipster trousers and a Boer War army tunic which was black with gold buttons and red braid. Walking around the dull, fine city of Norwich provoked the expected howls of derision, threats and insults, which is probably why I did it. Not being one of *them*, the brain-dead, carrot-crunching lager louts gave me comfort, made me think that one day, I could get out of the city, be something – anything – else. Most of the music I listened to was early psychedelia – Love, Pink Floyd with Syd, Zombies, Yardbirds. Modern life was too dull and predictable, so acid, dope and tripping to 'Interstellar Overdrive' seemed a good alternative. Then a filmmaker student friend of mine held me captive in his seething pit of a flat in Sheffield. It was raining all of the time, he and his new girlfriend spent all day and most of the night in bed. He only had new albums to listen to, but *The Queen is Dead* at least looked interesting, so I put it on. First, the psychedelia-swathed guitar workout of the title track captured my attention. And then this. As I listened, in my mind images of Harold Wilson, Bill Shankly, Norman Wisdom, Rita Tushingham, Susan George, Albert Finney and Tom Courtenay danced jigs in the cobbled streets of Manchester. It was pure *Saturday Night, Sunday Morning* or *Billy Liar*. It was so queerly 1960s in its naïve attitude. It isn't a sneer and a two-fingered salute, it's oddly polite and so wildly ambitious. Laugh? I nearly stopped smoking. Getting to know more about The Smiths thereafter brought me back to the modern world. I swapped the psychedelia for spotted shirts, a quiff and bunches of gladioli. The insults, threats and staring continued.

Girlfriend In A Coma

MELANIE NEWMAN of Brentwood, Essex

My very first Smiths song. I was idly watching *The Chart Show*, pretending to be doing some homework when there it was. Somehow different from anything I'd heard before, it nevertheless struck a chord. At that time, buried in trying to cope with being an 'odd one out', I didn't pursue it – the last thing I needed was yet another reason to be laughed at, another reason to be made to feel foolish. In any event, I knew the band were to split, so there didn't seem much point. Of course, had I made the *right* decision, the niche I so desperately craved would have appeared.

Perhaps it was meant to work out that way, for when I needed them most some years later I found them, but that first meeting still strikes me as rather ironic.

JULIE BALFOUR of London, N1

This will always remind me of my friend Sunayla's sixteenth birthday party. Hampstead Heath, getting very pissed and singing Smiths songs very loudly and very badly. Just having a generally good time.

But soon it's time to make off and catch the last train home. Problem! Sarah is unconscious. (She'd spent the last three hours fervently guzzling the 'house' cocktail of malibu, vodka and cider.) We can't move her so we attempt to roll her down the hill. It doesn't work, and in any case, the station lies up the hill. Before long, the hopelessness and gravity of our predicament hit home and we decide to visit a nearby house and phone an ambulance. The people, thankfully, are nice and the ambulance is duly called and Sarah is rushed off to hospital.

Meanwhile, drained of all *joie de vivre*, we trail homeward to await further news. At last – eventually – we find out that she's not dead but that she'd slipped in and out of a coma throughout the night. Sarah is discharged the next morning and we go and visit her, only to find that she hasn't even got a hangover.

Perhaps it was relief more than anything else which induced some bright spark to make the obvious lyrical adaptation.

MARK of St Albans, Hertfordshire

It's really very simple.

I remember the first time I heard Morrissey's voice. I was eleven years old. I was sitting downstairs by the television watching a pop music programme. 'Girlfriend In A Coma' came on. Morrissey's face appeared on the screen and I sat up. He was beautiful. The sounds he made were beautiful. From that moment on, there has been nobody else who can make me feel the way he did at that moment.

The song has stayed with me for a long time. Typical Morrissey: funny, flippant . . . beautiful. Today, I often wonder what would have happened if he had not been around to offer all that he has given me – how things would be different. That face, those eyes, that voice and that knowing look. He has given me a love that can't be equalled and I thank him for that.

It really is just that simple.

All Men Have Secrets

JENNY PARKIN of Huddersfield, West Yorkshire

It was the nice country-hotel wedding reception of two thirty-something barristers' clerks, somewhere dark and rural outside Leeds. The night was wearing off fast. The bridegroom, apparently, was sitting on the toilet, beer bottle in hand, pants round ankles and door wide open, telling random passers-by how they were his best fucking mate. His brother, the best man, had asked the DJ if he wanted a fight several hours before. The problem was that Peter, the bridegroom, had provided the DJ with a play-list which clearly stated that his interests stretched no further than The Stranglers and Wall Of Voodoo. But the DJ, a small man with a thin, reedy moustache and a rumpled white tuxedo, had seen fit to spin the worst of the current chart crop all night. I kept quiet, feeling a bit conspicuous. The best wedding outfit I'd been able to scare up consisted of darkish jeans without holes in, and a darkish T-shirt without beans down. I didn't even know the couple – I was only there with one of the office boys, at what was the beginning of a lovely relationship. The relatives of the couple and other respectable people had left long ago, leaving only the stalwart drinkers with a lot of empty bottles. By way of a peacemaking offer, the DJ pulled out 'Girlfriend In A Coma'. My new boyfriend and I shared the poxy parquet dancefloor with the happy couple, all flinging our arms about in true Smithsy fashion. Suddenly everything was just about right – me and my junior clerk, the cheesy disco lights, and Peter with a beery glint in his eye, challenging us to name the date.

JULIE BALFOUR of London, N1

This song also recalls my first meeting, some years ago, with Dennis, who has since become a good friend.

I was at a pretty grim party and became aware of people asking: 'Where's Dennis? Where's Dennis?' repeatedly. Hundreds and hundreds of times. 'Popular bloke,' I surmised. 'Must be either a wanker or a drugs dealer.'

But no – when this mystical character appeared, he cut an altogether different figure: tall, clumsy, camp and friendly looking to boot. And wearing a 'Meat Is Murder' T-shirt.

I introduced myself immediately and we proceeded to monopolise the stereo for the entire evening, playing *Strangeways* . . . among numerous other Smiths gems. Aside from this, we enthused at length about the band, and kept half an eye on the wankers who were hell-bent on setting fire to Dennis's T-shirt.

Instant friends, with missionary zeal we played this song over and over to show that, 'No, really, it's not depressing at all, and really quite funny if you listen properly.'

They didn't believe us.

MIKE CAMPBELL of Giffnock, Glasgow

Due to financial considerations, summer 1987's holiday had to be cheap and cheerful. At the last moment myself and the lads were offered the free use of a workmate's family holiday apartment in Santa Ponsa, Majorca. Problem solved. Two weeks in the Spanish sun instead of the proposed ten days in Bournemouth or some other idyllic location.

Having checked in at Glasgow airport we noticed that amidst all our trendy apparel lurked the most hideous pair of shoes we had ever seen. This disgusting footwear belonged to none other than Stephen Bisset, one of the lads more noted for his Mr Fixit capabilities than his (questionable) fashion sense. Poor Bisset was berated from the word go. Comparisons with long deceased grandmothers' footwear abounded. Resilient to the last, Bisset instructed us to piss off and worry about our own problems. 'Fair enough, Granny,' said I, safe in the knowledge that I was the coolest thing since Frankie said 'Relax'.

It had been my job to prepare the sounds for the trip. I had puzzled over what would be appropriate for some time before. I decided that three tapes would be in order – Mike's Majorca Mega-Mix parts, I, II, and III. The tapes mainly comprised the popular groups of the time. Hipsway, Love And Money and The Big Dish were all popular up Glasgow way and, as all young shavers like to do, the boys wanted something cooked up that stamped 'Glaswegians Abroad' on our holiday in the sun. Said task was duly completed and the tapes, at our hastily-arranged parties, went down a storm.

All except one song that is. A major *faux pas* on my part was to sandwich 'Girlfriend In A Coma' between Spagna's 'Call Me' and Baltimora's 'Tarzan Boy'. When the party was in full swing, Moz would suddenly start belting out, usually to silence and much shuffling of feet. The guys present were infidels to a man and the last thing they needed to hear was a reminder of their better half back in Blighty or Holland or Ireland or wherever. As you can imagine, the fast-forward button was almost immediately pressed with some venom and the wheels of the party would once again plough slowly into motion.

Our apartment was on the ground floor and the view from the window was of some massive bushes. There was this constant problem of flies and bugs attaching themselves to the nearest nourishing body as a result of which we would spend much of the day lying in an extremely drunken stupor, sweating like mad. Unless someone stood guard at the window it had to remain shut. Unfortunately on one occasion bug security was somewhat remiss and it is with startling clarity that I remember the consequences.

Myself, Ned and Paul had taken a considerable cargo of *cerveza* to the beach, drained the lot and repaired to a local hostelry for a top-up. In the sweltering afternoon heat we began to feel a bit tired and emotional and decided to grab a couple of hours sleep before the real revelry began later that night. It must have been about 100°C in the apartment so we decided that the window *had* to be opened and to hell with the consequences. We were so drunk that it didn't occur to us just how hateful the contents of Pandora's Box might be.

We must have been snoozing for about ten minutes when I was awakened by a fleet of maverick flies or mosquitoes intent on sucking the very lifeblood from me. As you know, swatting buzzing insects and getting some shut-eye do not mix, so, heaving myself out of my drowsy, inebriated sleep, I reached for a magazine to dispose of the pests. It was then I realised that we were not alone.

Clinging to the ceiling was a locust. Not just any old locust but a LOCUST! I didn't want to move just in case this winged leviathan attempted to savage me. Using the magazine I poked and prodded the other two lads awake. Spagna began blaring from the cassette recorder but I didn't want to disturb the locust's obvious liking for Euro disco. Spagna blared on as we retreated warily to the door. Safety had nearly been reached when in burst Bisset, flushed from his success at beating Derek in a pool competition. If it's at all possible, he managed to slam the door *open*. Bang! The locust sprang on to the floor looking decidedly belligerent. 'What's the problem?' enquired Bisset, bemused at our frozen positions. We informed him of the plight in hand to which his reply was, 'No bother chaps, leave it to me.' He walked over to The Great Beast, removed one of his corduroy platform shoes and beat it with one swift whack to an unrecognisable pulp. There was much disdain at Bisset's cavalier disposal of the creature, but he was not to be cheated out of his second victory in as many minutes. 'Nobody messes with the abominable shoe man,' he cried, arms aloft. Alarmed and perhaps a little wary of such a radical change in such a reserved guy we backed out of the door sheepishly. The tape rumbled on and as Morrissey whispered his last goodbyes we knew it was really serious.

Girl Afraid

VIRGINIE CHENNEREAU of Blois, France

During the school year 1986 I met a guy named Sammy. We got on really well and I also met his friends – Jean, Chris, Birdy and two others (I can't remember their names). We all became good friends. At this time I was already a fan of The Smiths, but thought Morrissey a little bit sorrowful.

My new friends took me to different places and parties where (of course!) we'd listen to The Smiths and other bands. To go to those parties we had a car with only four seats, but there were about six or seven of us and I was the only girl. We were all around eighteen years old, and would scream 'Girl Afraid' – feeling very hotheaded and not very sober. I suppose it was dangerous driving like that when we were so excited, but it was so funny. We'd take hours and hours to get back home for what was only a journey of 20 or 30 km. Unfortunately Jean is not here with us anymore. He is dead. Sammy is far from where I live and I don't know anymore about the others. But when I listen to 'Girl Afraid' or The Smiths in general, I think always of those nice times.

LAURENCE HOPE of St Helier, Jersey

The wind snapped like a greased bullwhip. Crack! It came from nowhere. Her eyes flickered briefly, before closing once more.

The hypnotic push-me-pull-me of a late tide rocks a coastal evening to sleep. The town grows quiet around this time. The ebb and flow of daytime giving ground to the crackle, spit and boom of night. Thump, thump, thump – the clarion call of the disco dollies. Casting one eye over my shoulder, I see the pub door open. Thump, THUMP, THUMP, thump. Its human flotsam seems to beckon, frown and thumb a spiteful nose at me and mine. I don't need them as much as they don't need me. All square and not a blow landed. Fair enough.

She wakes and instinctively nuzzles the collar of my old coat. Sea-spray sits in little bubbles on her hair and dapples its pink ribbon. The weather is dreadful, but then, this *is* August.

'But is this love or is it Memorex?' I ask myself. I feel loss when she goes to buy a newspaper. I AM the boy afraid, but fearful of exactly what? The powder blue railings sparkle and glisten save for those patches where the valiant efforts of council painters have yielded to oxidation. Gently, I shake her awake. 'Will you marry me?' I whisper. 'Are you asking?' she replies, smiling her smile, stifling a yawn. Picking up, gratefully, on her mischievousness, I reply that there seems nothing much better to do in this salty hellhole. 'But I've got to meet my boyfriend at the airport tomorrow morning.'

Six years on and I've never seen her since. I walk down that way every now and again with a packet of sandwiches and a bottle of Vimto. I can smell her hair and her clothes and her Rothmans yet. I raise a bottle to them and to seaside holiday romance.

Half A Person

MATTHEW FREESTONE of Bexleyheath, Kent

This song recalls August 1989 when I attended a Smiths convention in Manchester. I cannot claim to have enjoyed the evening wholeheartedly, and in truth it probably marked the end of my time as a true fan of the band.

On arrival, I found the hall filled with small cliques who had either arrived together or formed early on. Being alone and somewhat shy, I tried to talk to several people in an attempt to be sociable, but found a coldness which was both surprising and hugely disappointing. I don't doubt that there were people present who'd have been more welcoming, but sadly we weren't fated to meet that night.

As for the entertainment, the video show seemed amateurish, the coach trip trivial and vile in retrospect and the club itself reminded me of a hothouse – sweaty with warmth and moisture and strewn with flowers. Despite all this, I half enjoyed myself. With so much Smiths paraphernalia around, I could hardly have done otherwise.

Almost without knowing it, I was slowly growing out of The Smiths. But it's also true that without them, I might never have made it so far.

RUTH of Mitcham, Surrey

I cannot claim to have spent 'six long years' on Morrissey's trail (not literally, at least!), but this song does recall one frantic

43 duke street
1/1

, Kshoil, muth, milk thistle

evening spent pursuing him around London.

A friend of mine called me excitedly one afternoon to report that Morrissey would be appearing on *The Jonathan Ross Show* at teatime. He'd heard the news on *Steve Wright in the Afternoon*. Knowing Wright's well-documented dislike of Morrissey, I remained slightly sceptical and loath to build my hopes up, but tuned in none the less.

I was only half-watching when Jonathan began to introduce the next guest with trademark flippancy: 'Here's a man whose recent songs include "Hairdresser On Fire" and "Tony The Pony".' If my attention was now fully focused, I still smelled some kind of a rat due to the mocking introduction. However, seconds later there he was, performing 'I've Changed My Plea To Guilty' and my lingering doubts vanished.

I called my friend as soon as the song finished and we decided to make for the studios in the (slim!) hope of meeting him. Morrissey, that is, not Jonathan Ross. We reached the Channel 4 studios flustered and anxious only to discover that we were in the wrong place and that the show was made at London Bridge. Now we knew that our chances of seeing Morrissey had all but disappeared, but carried on regardless. Our persistence that night must have rivalled Jason's pursuit of the Golden Fleece! Two hours later found us in the right place only to learn that we'd missed our quarry by a mere fifteen minutes.

But a strange thing happened *en route*. That part of London is dark, dingy and shot-through with creepy little alleys – 'historic', the brochures would label it. In approaching the studios, we got hopelessly lost and not knowing where the hell we were, found ourselves on Bermondsey Street of 'Last Of The Famous International Playboys' fame!

NORMAN CUMMINS of Govan, Glasgow

Been there, done this . . . ! Chasing a girl throughout secondary school and getting absolutely nowhere. I recall trying desperately to find out where she lived, but no one seemed to know quite where – only the general neighbourhood. So many a summer night was spent running up and down closes, inspecting the nameplates. I eventually did the sensible thing and followed her home. Sensible thing? God, what a plonker!

RACHEL RANDALL of Nuneaton, Warwickshire

A pleasant, pastoral, but poorly-executed canvas of Olde Englande – Constable's *The Haywain* fourteen times removed.

We lived in the same house until I was twenty: the kind of unremarkable near-clone semi in which much of Britain's moderately-well-to-do shake down of an evening. It's now eight years since the move, but I still remember every wall and every surface and every corner of every room. Perhaps I'm not alone in thinking that those household objects upon which our child-ish eyes fall a million times are somehow destined to remain potently evocative and totem-like. Jugs, jars, books, pictures.

The picture in question hung halfway up the staircase high above my head, gradually lowering itself to around shoulder-height over a period of fifteen years. Over the same timespan it degenerated somewhat from the most magical, artistic realisa-tion ever to a rather scratchy and naff old dud. Truly, this picture had a life of its own! Sure, the artist may once have been famous and venerated, but for rugby league or poultry hus-bandry or somesuch – it certainly wasn't for painting.

But my story and my memories and this song owe much to the man or woman responsible. A man or woman whose grace-ful if bizarre signature appeared in slim brown strokes in the bottom left corner – next to an old plough. It wasn't any old signature and bore greater resemblance to a mathematical for-mula than a human handle. For twenty years, hardly a day must have passed without my peering and puzzling and wondering who might '1/2AP' have been? The answer, of course, like so many others, arrived with The Smiths.

MARIAN COLE of Brooklyn, New York, USA

Going to London in '93 was certainly the best thing that has ever happened to me. I'd wanted to go since I was thirteen, when punk showed up in stark relief just how boring and backward my home-town really was. And all those great bands were from London! Well, better late than never . . . By the time I *did* arrive, I was accompanied by my 'London' music collection, in which Smiths tapes featured prominently. This song was the first one committed to it. Next time, it's Manchester.

Hand In Glove

ANDREW TAYLOR of Bootle, Liverpool

I was fortunate enough (understatements, eh?) to meet Morrissey in Liverpool during the 'Meat Is Murder' tour. As he was signing my album sleeve, I blurted out the question he must have heard a million times before: 'What's your favourite Smiths song?' He answered, ' "Hand In Glove", what's yours?' 'It's mine, too,' I stammered back, and we proceeded to chat about the tour and how much he liked that evening's supporting guests, James. Morrissey then signed my copy of that week's *NME*, bearing a cover picture of his protégés. I treasure it to this day: 'I love James . . . Morrissey X.'

LEE HARRISON of Heworth, Yorkshire

I get really vexed when people accuse The Smiths of being the most miserable band ever. Sure, like most fans I've found solace in the words and music when depressed, but for me The Smiths have shone on some of the happiest and most carefree days of my life.

Almost every Smiths song has a special place in my heart but this one evokes a year I spent in Toulouse, France – so far from all that I knew and loved. Initially, I felt quite alone and, as usual, turned to The Smiths for comfort: in this case, something quintessentially English in a foreign environment. Slowly, however, the feelings of isolation were replaced by a warm sense of home and belonging which I could never have anticipated. As The Smiths echoed through the corridors of the university residence in which I lived, my life became filled with the most wonderful people I will ever meet. We had the most insane and most enjoyable of times.

On reflection, I suppose we were *all* outsiders coming to grips with a system which felt like someone else's. In effect, we created our own little world – living like brothers and sisters with the sound of The Smiths ever present, day and night. I was appointed teacher of lyrics and interpreter of the more obscure passages. We reeled around the fountain wearing only our underwear and sang songs while walking into town, oblivious to the strange looks we attracted. And someone, somewhere, has a recording of the most unmelodious version of 'Panic' ever heard, bellowed into a soy sauce bottle smuggled from the canteen.

One day, of course, our fantasy world had to come to an end and that which I'd built around me and come to love so dearly had to be dismantled. On a sunny June day my posters came down from the walls and joined my records in the waiting suitcases, ready once more for dear old Blighty. The room now bare and forbidding – no longer home – my best friend Vincent was still nowhere to be seen but I waited and waited, intent on singing The Smiths just one more time. Then, as 'Back To The Old House' played for the umpteenth time that night, in he staggered, drunk, and hugged me. He dragged me outside, and standing on the bridge over the Canal du Midi we wailed 'Hand In Glove' at three in the morning. We both knew that it would never be quite the same again. For that short period of our lives, the sun *had* shone from our behinds and our love *hadn't* been like any other.

No doubt most people read this song as a tale of two lovers; for us, it became symbolic of a deep and lasting friendship. Happiness found in the hardest of times. Out of our sadness grew the madness which spawned a thousand crazy days and crazier nights. The Smiths were a central part of that and if the people stared, then the people stared – we really didn't know and we really didn't care.

ANGIE J. LEWIS of Huddersfield, Yorkshire

The Smiths convention of 1990 in Manchester is the memory that springs to mind every time I hear 'Hand In Glove'. I went down on my own from Huddersfield, and I left on my own. I hardly talked to anyone while I was there. But do you know what? It didn't really matter all that much (even though I felt pretty lonely) because I had The Smiths on my side, and no one could (or can, to this day) take them away from me. My parents hated The Smiths, my friends did too, but I didn't care. I was, and still am, immensely proud of them, and me and The Lads were (and still are) *definitely* like no other love I've ever had. As a result, I was entirely defiant, even at the convention where a lot of people avoided and/or ignored me (probably and possibly because I don't have a three-foot quiff and am of West Indian origin – *not* your 'typical' Smiths fan!). It's not been at all easy being a Smiths fan because a lot of people have found it unusual (even wrong) due to the fact that I happen to be black – and so what if I am? But then, 'If the people stare, let the people stare'. After all, 'What difference does it make?'

SIMON LANE of Winterbourne, Avon

Reminds me of leaving Dover on the cross-channel ferry. Watching the white cliffs disappear in sea mist to the sound of a quintessentially English song.

KARIN DRUPPERS of Utrecht, Holland

The first time I heard The Smiths was in 1986 and the song was this one. At that time I used to often visit a club called Switch

– a place (the only one in Utrecht) known for its alternative music. Morrissey's warm and special voice attracted me immediately.

My sister and I quickly set about buying up all The Smiths LPs and in no time were up to date with everything they'd ever done and were doing. That music was to give us a special bond and a kind of private world which we share to this day through the albums and articles and concerts and Smiths/Morrissey nights in Amsterdam.

Sadly, Switch is no more, but its legacy remains precious for two Dutch Smiths fans at least.

The Hand That Rocks The Cradle

MATT MILLER of Cody, Wyoming, USA

There was a place we had dubbed 'Kerbytown' just south of where I lived while at high school. It wasn't a town at all but a dry ravine between two white hillsides mined for gypsum. There, at Kerbytown, three of us – Dave, Cohen and myself – would gather for adolescent drinking binges and exchanges of that seemingly banal conversation which becomes more intense and more important with the passing of each year. We'd play Smiths tapes in Dave's dashboard. 'The Hand That Rocks The Cradle' held us spellbound in this eerie, isolated place. I think most music reminds a person of when they first heard it, but the music of The Smiths – this is what we *were*.

ADRIAN HOWARTH of Sale, Cheshire

This song brings to mind an embarrassing incident from the summer of 1984. It ought to have been a time of O level revision, but how can you revise when you've just fallen in love? 'Two Tribes' was at number one for months, and the sun shone forever. Perhaps this accounted for a drastic improvement in my spots, although cutting down on masturbation might also have been a factor. She was my first proper girlfriend and even though we hadn't 'done' anything yet, I lived in hope.

Anyway, a friend of mine threw a party one Thursday night. My birthday. And so with a bit of strategic fibbing, this was to be IT. Our first night together. Well, it was and it wasn't . . . I lay awake for hours paralysed with fear while she slept soundly. We made a surreptitious exit at 6 a.m. for fear of imminent parental arrival and wandered around the park for two hours before catching the bus into town. First on the birthday shopping list was the album. *The Smiths*. We returned to my bedroom at 10 a.m. to play it and see whatever else might ensue. I placed it on the turntable, lay on the bed beside her and promptly fell asleep. Fatigue had prevailed over nervous energy. The Hand That Rocks The Cradle.

DOMINIC LAWSON of Hemel Hempstead, Hertfordshire

It was 1984, and I was eleven. Voluntarily estranged from my peers and consumed with acne. I'd sought solace in the first three Smiths singles – each an unexpected delight and much needed respite from Wham! and Nik Bastard Kershaw.

At last, here was pop music of real worth, free of the usual class gimmicks and light years away from the graceless pretension of the highly mediocre indie scene of the times. Alone in my bedroom, my first listen to The Smiths was an unprecedented joyous event: shiver down the spine, hairs on the back of my neck standing to attention, lump in the throat, the whole lot. Ten beautiful, timeless songs, making an already fairly happy child a great deal happier. Most of all, 'The Hand That Rocks The Cradle' – sheer fucking poetry set to the most heartbreaking music I'd ever heard – brought tears of wonder and relief to my eyes. Only three songs have ever made me blub in such a manner, and two of them by The Smiths. Rapture lay ahead, of course; so many impossibly great songs, still unsurpassed at any time before or since. Every release, a landmark in my teenage life, as The Smiths pissed from a great height on every contemporary, every song and every press favourite, past or present. Champions!

Ten years later as I bellow feebly along to those songs, it's deeply satisfying to have felt part of something which touched so many of us, something so culturally spectacular, and yet so intensely personal. What lucky sods we were.

CHARLOTTE HALL of Leith, Edinburgh

At school my friend and I used to have lyric competitions, designed to show off our encyclopædic knowledge of Smiths songs. We developed a code for referring to people we disliked by using quotes. Thus, 'She's annoying the shit out of me,' would become the sage comment, 'There'll be blood on the cleaver tonight.'

Handsome Devil

JOAN CANAL OLIVERAS of Manresa, Spain

When I listen to 'Handsome Devil', I am reminded of my college years when I'd tutor primary school children to earn some pocket money. There was this eleven- or twelve-year-old blonde girl with piercing blue eyes. She was to become my private Lolita, the entrancing nymphette who switched from one position to another constantly: one moment truly learning, the next misbehaving on purpose and asking to be punished, the next complaining . . . We had quite a weird game between us, the meaning of which I was too young to fully understand. At the time I saw her as a fallen angel but now I realise she was a handsome devil.

MELANIE NEWMAN of Brentwood, Essex

Sitting in a cramped converted attic, with the smell of the newly-opened Tandoori making me feel decidedly queasy and listening to a scratchy tape of instructions backed up by a manual which was as dull as it looked, I learned to type. Not such a remarkable feat I suppose, but this is how I spent most of the summer of '92 after failing more GCSEs than I thought I would a year or so previously. The ensuing qualifications took me through one dead-end job in a mobile phone shop and several stuffy civil service jobs in the capital, none of which I really enjoyed or even felt satisfied in. So, quitting the world of work, I decided to become a student once more and try for some A levels (formal qualifications are usually waived for mature students at my HE college). However, that wasted summer of '92 finally held some meaning this year when, after meeting the boys behind the book a few months previously, I began typing up the edited material for *All Men Have Secrets*. I suppose I'll forgive them for handing me the first 20,000 words on the back of cornflake packets, used betting slips and the like, even though the whole lot fell off my desk one night and had to be retrieved, re-sorted and each one marked off against the printout. I'll forgive them for the envelopes containing 500 to 1,000 words each which poured daily through my letterbox and which I would read in lectures, thus missing details of homework assignments and getting it in the neck for not paying attention. However, I will thank them for the convenient excuse to listen to my Smiths albums again while typing the whole lot up. (One can hardly listen to anything else having embarked on such a project, although I don't really *need* an excuse to give an old friend a listening.) I especially listened to *Hatful of Hollow*, being my favourite (which I'd lent to a friend for a couple of months, and got back the day before I started the job).

Above my desk, on the ceiling, is my favourite picture of Morrissey. It was positioned there to console me if, during essay writing, I turned my eyes heavenwards for inspiration. It is a black and white poster of him lying on a bed, wearing a cosy-looking jumper, with an Oscar Wilde book peeking out from underneath his arm. As I type, I can imagine him looking benevolently down, watching my efforts, and perhaps even having a giggle at some of the stories. Well, Moz, if you are reading this, let me just say that you really are *the* handsomest devil, and if it wasn't for you I would have been in bed hours ago.

The Headmaster Ritual

ANDREW TAYLOR of Bootle, Liverpool

The release day of *Meat is Murder* found me most perturbed, being without the necessary funds to go out and grab a copy. Luckily, my friend Graham Horley possessed the financial wherewithal and had wasted little time in obtaining one. The Horley family lived at the side of our house, on the corner of the next road, and the window of the bedroom Graham shared with his brother Jeff was visible from my own. I whistled (our calling signal) and shouted 'Have you got *Meat is Murder* yet?' God knows what the neighbours must've thought of this. Yes. Graham had indeed bought the album, so I made haste round the corner and listened through twice without stopping for breath. For me, the immediate standout track was the opener and it will always remind me of leaning out the window hollering a question which would've been unintelligible to anyone but a Smiths fan. Some weeks later, my parents went off leaving me in charge at home. Graham asked if he could stay over during their absence and I said yes – but only if he brought the album.

NORMAN CUMMINS of Govan, Glasgow

The teachers at Govan High School, save for a few honourable exceptions. Also, teenage get-togethers where the sound of The

Smiths was met with the traditional wrist-slashing simulation by those assembled. I found this song surprisingly lively and enjoyable, but didn't have the nerve to say so. I would now.

SOPHIE LEGENCHE of Neuville-Sur-Oise, France

It happened a few years ago: it was a Sunday morning and already the dreadful thought of having to return to school the next day throws me into a brooding and sulky mood. The day is spoilt. Was it really that awful? Yes indeed, for it meant having to see again the same mean faces and having to sit still writing down what some highbrow, moralising person wanted us to think. No doubt they knew the ritual by heart. I cannot bear the 'Almighty General' rule, for it makes no provision for the needs of the individual, thus leaving behind thousands of people – those who are invariably branded 'misfits'. Those who rebel are too often regarded as 'pretentious peacocks', when in fact they have merely become aware of the tragedy of conformity and have elected to flee at maximum speed. The songs of The Smiths always seemed to me to endorse this brave decision and 'The Headmaster Ritual' sums up what for many young people, is the first inkling of the problems to come ...

Heaven Knows I'm Miserable Now

PHILLIP MORRIS of Warrington, Cheshire

It was on a Tuesday evening in the summertime of 1984 that my destiny was determined in three-and-a-half minutes of wondrousness. I had just completed another tedious day at the office performing menial tasks. Feeling depressed, all I wanted to do was go out, get intoxicated and forget for a while the meaningless banality of life. Then this song came on the chart run-down and things took on a whole new perspective. Tomorrow, I thought to myself, I will indeed spit in the eye of my boss and present two defiant fingers to this humdrum society.

Sadly, I am now 29 years of age with no job, no money and few prospects. I do, however, still have The Smiths, fond memories and inner peace.

ADRIAN HOWARTH of Sale, Cheshire

It quickly became apparent from talking to friends and classmates that when it came to The Smiths there was no middle ground. You either loved them or hated them. The vast majority of people I knew fell into the latter category. To them, The Smiths were just a bunch of miserable bastards, and they regarded this song as conclusive proof of that.

Weekly, without fail, this hatred was vented in the woodwork class. It became their custom to recreate *Scum* by forcing me into the woodstore and hitting me with pieces of dowling until I a) did up the top button of my shirt, b) spat on my shoes to clean them and c) admitted The Smiths were shit and that 'Driving In My Car' by Madness was the greatest popular song ever recorded.

When the subject of psychological bullying is discussed in the press and on television, I know exactly what they mean. Being hit with lengths of wood was nothing compared with having to admit that Madness were better than The Smiths.

IAIN KEY of Cheadle, Cheshire

I was in Jamaica last year. As we landed in Montego Bay it was 38 degrees and this was playing in the taxi from the airport. Over the fortnight, The Smiths were played as much as Bob Marley or UB40. Our taxi driver, Courtney, demanded a copy of my compilation and was playing it full blast when last seen.

TOM GALLAGHER of Giffnock, Glasgow

Gran's death in the last days of June '84 coincided with the beginning of a freak heatwave in which Scotland would bake for the next five weeks. It was the first truly distressing event of my hitherto untroubled seventeen years. And yet the awful, gnawing sense of loss was tempered with some small measure of relief; her timing could hardly have been more convenient.

The months before had seen my finger placed firmly on the self-destruct button, the most tangible evidence of which would shortly drop through the letterbox in the shape of my Higher Grade certificate. I awaited the day entirely without suspense, secure in the knowledge that it would record an 'A' in Higher English and nothing else. I had resolved to do so abominably in all other subjects so as to obtain what were commonly referred to as 'non-mentions'. If this was hardly the most arduous of assignments, it did, perversely, demand some measure of bravery, since my Ordinary Grade certificate of twelve months earlier displayed 'A' bands in all subjects. Incidentally, the word 'bravery' appears in its little-used context of 'risible, middle-class, adolescent posturing'. Gran, I'm sure, would have taken no part in the ructions which inevitably followed but would have been deeply hurt none the less. She belonged to that precious strain of the Scottish working-class which prized excellence in all its forms and regarded academic achievement as being wonderfully, joyously consistent with its instinctive socialism. But now she was gone and I was devastated but at least fire-breathing parents would be a doddle by comparison ...

Circumstances dictated that – for the very first time – I would spend several weeks alone in the house. With my Smiths obsession approaching its first birthday I took the opportunity to play, and replay, the twenty or so tracks then committed to vinyl. Idling in the sun, the cigarette habit with which I had furtively flirted was fully consummated.

'Heaven Knows I'm Miserable Now' was released in May of that year. Whether heaven knew it or not, I certainly was, but the sense of magic remains with me to this day. The magic of the song and the magic of The Smiths. On hearing that deep, resonant opening or on seeing the grey and orange of the sleeve, pungent memories flood back of a time when The Smiths meant EVERYTHING ... and then some.

CRAIG SOWERBY of Coquitlam, BC, Canada

I guess my story begins back in June, around the time I first became aware of *All Men Have Secrets* and wrote off to Scotland for details. I had recently graduated from university, but was unemployed and stuck living with my parents and spending a great deal of time with my Smiths collection. I suppose my mood would have been best encapsulated by 'Heaven Knows I'm Miserable Now'. Then, without prior warning or notice, I enjoyed what appeared to be the most incredible stroke of luck . . .

A pretty, nineteen-year-old Belgian girl was sent to spend the summer with me. Why? She was the daughter of my father's business associate and needed to improve her English in 'preparation for an exam. I would be her 'mentor' in these endeavours, while both of us worked for Dad's company. She arrived at the beginning of July. Her name was Amaya and her English *was* pretty poor. As it happens, I'm fairly fluent in French, so that immediately became the language in which we conversed. We hit it off at once and before long couldn't bear to be apart. On her very first Friday in Canada, my parents took her to their summer cottage, intent on spending the weekend there. Originally, I had no plans to leave the city, but by Saturday morning was taking the ferry to be with her. I think she must have been the happiest girl in the world when she woke up to find me eating breakfast in the kitchen.

I have never, in my 23 years, known anyone with whom I connected in such a way. She was the first person I wanted to see in the morning and the last person I wanted to see before falling asleep at night. That she had a boyfriend back home, initially of little importance, inevitably began to loom large in our thoughts. One day, she asked me if I'd want her as my girlfriend if she lived in Vancouver. I replied that I'd want her as my girlfriend if she lived on the far side of the moon. So with that, we became a 'couple', and things got even better. I finally felt that luck had smiled on me – that fate had brought me the most special girl in all the world.

At this point I should say that The Smiths and Morrissey quickly became our soundtrack of the summer. She had never heard of The Smiths and was only vaguely aware of Morrissey, but grew to like the music so much that his was soon the only voice to be heard from my car stereo.

Around this time, Amaya's father offered me a year-long job setting up a new computer system at a factory he owns in Spain, despite the fact that he was reportedly angry about the time we were spending whispering lovers' confidences – and these in French, not English. Her father is a very dominating man, and I suppose it came as no surprise to learn of his disapproval of what would constitute unforgiveable behaviour for a young Catholic girl. This, added to her increasing guilt over cheating on her boyfriend, meant that there was an air of inevitability about the end to our happiness. The day she broke up with me brought painful emotions of anger and sorrow. I really hadn't seen it coming, as perhaps I should. So blinded was I by pure euphoria that the undoubted awkwardness of her position barely crossed my mind. In the event, I decided that it would be silly and perverse to hate this girl when we could still have so much fun as friends. Establishing things on this different footing didn't take long since our compatibility was so manifestly obvious.

The next weekend she was invited by a friend of my father's to join him and his daughter on their yacht. I was not invited, and it proved to be the longest weekend of my life as I retreated to the summer cottage for a little solitude and a lot of Smiths. I needed her presence so badly – be it as a lover or friend. On her return, she appeared as happy as I was to be together again. At a disco that evening I thought I'd seen the look in her eyes that said, 'I want you to kiss me,' but avoided doing so, assuming some mistake on my part. But the next day, she told me that some hard thinking on the boat had convinced her that we should be a couple once more. Naïvely, we resolved not to get too serious this time – we'd just 'fool around' until the time came for her to return to Belgium and her boyfriend.

The following two weeks were perhaps the happiest of my life, since I'd found someone in whom I had supreme confidence to share most anything with. We went to clubs, soccer matches, baseball games, amusement parks and of course the cottage – most of the time hand in hand. But the best moments were those hidden away, in one another's arms, exploring our likes and dislikes and sharing our deepest secrets.

Then our world self-destructed. Her father, now convinced

that the Canadian experiment was not working, called to summon her home immediately. Thoughts of hopping a plane to Las Vegas and eloping were quickly dismissed and she boarded one, instead, for Brussels. On landing, Amaya called me to say that she'd caused quite a stir *en route* by crying for most of the ten-hour flight. Neither of us knew what to do. I even went to a travel agency hoping to buy a ticket to Europe. It transpired that the only flight within my budget would not leave for a week – I would certainly have been on one departing that day. Over the phone, I told her that I would follow her in a short time, but would do so on the understanding that we got married, since such a course of action would anger both our families so much that we'd have effectively 'burnt our boats'. I left her with that proposal until the following day. My plan was to accept her father's job offer in Spain, from where I would be able to visit her on a semi-regular basis. If, after a year, we were still of the same mind I would enrol for a Masters programme at her university in order that we could be together. After that, marriage would be inevitable.

Things started getting a bit rocky when we discussed my visiting her prior to taking up the Spanish appointment. She was still fearful of her father finding out about us before being given the opportunity to 'vet' me as a worthy suitor for his daughter. With this, I began to get the first inklings of the end of our dream. Sure enough a fax arrived saying that she would prefer us to revert to being friends and correspondents. Suffice it to say that I was grievously hurt; we'd been discussing marriage one day only for her to suggest remaining penpals the next. The feeling that the one person I really, truly loved and cared for was betraying me cut so very deep. After a while I wrote to her saying that perhaps, one day, we could be friends but it would take some time for my broken heart to heal.

That was all several months ago. My job in Spain is still on hold – I've been plagued by visa problems at every turn. Sometimes I think I'm living in limbo: unable to find someone new because of my impending departure for Spain, and unable to persuade her to write to me very often. 'I'm a poor, freezingly cold soul/So far from where I intended to go.'

And another thing I can't do is listen to The Smiths much anymore. Jagged shards of memory spring from so many songs: 'Bigmouth . . .' and how I used to call her 'Sweetness'. The kisses we shared are recaptured by 'Still Ill'. And so the wheel has turned full circle. 'Two lovers entwined, pass me by, and heaven knows I'm miserable now . . .'

HELENE LE MELLOT of Lannion, France

In June '92 I was sitting the final part of my 'Bac', which is the French equivalent of A levels. I had to travel to a bigger town one day which was where the oral tests were being held. On returning, I was exhausted and felt terrible because I was really not confident at all in what I had done. So much seemed to hang on it: all through school, the teachers had built us up for that exam by saying that it would mark the end of childhood and the beginning of real life. I had the feeling that I'd spoiled seventeen years in one day!

My brother had recently returned from England where he'd bought several records. There, on the *Louder Than Bombs* CD, I found this song and immersed myself in it. In the event, I passed the exam with distinction, but that didn't change my fondness for the song at all!

EDUARDO CUERVO of Oviedo, Spain

This is the song of my life. Why? Because it changed it!

Everything happened when my life was a boring and clumsy one. It was summertime and I was always at home because I had no friends. I was alone and always doing what other people expected me to do. The only thing that cheered me up was a radio programme, *El Expreso de Medianoche* where the DJ played new records of new groups which weren't yet known in our country.

The first time he played this song I was shocked because it sounded so sad that I was not sure whether I liked it or not. But about a month later, the night I felt most depressed, I heard it again and, yes, that sad voice went directly to my soul. I recorded it and tried to understand it. That song reflected what I felt.

From that moment on I changed the way I was living my life and became the person I wanted to be, because as the song said: 'In my life why do I give valuable time to people who don't care if I live or die?'

After that, I found the album in London and I listened to it again and again, especially this song. It was then I decided to study English philology at the university because I had to learn English in order to understand what Morrissey sang.

Thanks to the cover of my folder I met other 'Smithsonians' at the university. Why? Because I had a sticker on the cover which said 'The Smiths' and I knew I was not alone anymore.

So, The Smiths saved my life and I'm really grateful to the DJ who played them during that horrible summer.

ANGIE J. LEWIS of Huddersfield, Yorkshire

Before I moved down to Manchester from my native Huddersfield to go to college, I used to hold down several dead-end office jobs. I was a VDU operator and worked as a very poorly paid office junior on the side. Making cups of tea for ungrateful recipients was *not* my idea of fun, I can tell you. But most of my work involved sending out CDs to places, so I was at least able to play some decent music a great deal of the time. I can remember travelling on the bus to Batley in West Yorkshire, with my walkman on, listening to 'Heaven Knows . . .' and being able to fully appreciate what Morrissey was lamenting. Even though I was 'lucky' enough to be working, and wasn't on the scrapheap or unemployed, I still totally despised my jobs and (a great deal of) the people I worked with. Most of my fellow employees were so tedious, and didn't seem to have any zest for life at all which I found quite frustrating. It was obvious where they were going to be in ten years' time, which is quite frightening really. And also, the fact that I earned a pittance didn't help matters either. I would probably rather have been unemployed, because then at least I wouldn't have had to be nice to people I didn't like very much. So it was a relief when I was made redundant from my last job before starting college, because it gave me a couple of months of freedom, during which I just bummed around at home as well as going down to London for a week during the time of Morrissey's infamous Finsbury Park appearance (I was there, and it wasn't an experience I'd like to repeat in a hurry!). But every time I hear 'Heaven Knows . . .' I remember those awful jobs and horrible people, and manage to *smile*.

NEIL MURRAY of Kelvinside, Glasgow

My first experience of The Smiths came during the summer of '84. As a youthful eleven year old playing snooker in my friend's garden with this song blaring out, I suppose life couldn't have been much rosier. Then came the news that one of our circle of friends had been killed climbing an electricity pylon. Although a special song to me, it still evokes memories of the death of our friend that summer.

CHRIS PRICE of Wolverhampton

Cushing's disease (or syndrome) affects only three people in every million, of which two-thirds are female, so I can honestly lay claim to being one in a million. Stemming from problems in the pituitary gland, common symptoms include moon face, obesity and a humped back. No disease can beat Cushing's when it comes to aesthetic displeasure! 'Heaven Knows I'm Miserable Now' was my anthem in the dark days and will remain so even now that things are really looking up. With the disease it doesn't matter what you do, who you're with or how good the surroundings – you constantly feel 'one degree under'.

DALE BROOKS of Alfreton, Derbyshire

Down Rock City, Nottingham. Just seen a crap gig by Sheep On Drugs which I've been dragged along to. Student night has now kicked in and I'm watching them all get very merry on pints at 50p a time. I'd join them if I wasn't driving. 'Heaven Knows . . .' comes on, interrupting the flow of dodgy dance and indie pop crap but finishes as abruptly as it started. Time to go home.

How Soon Is Now?

GAYE HUTCHINSON of Maltby, South Yorkshire

Sitting drunk in an empty pub in Cleethorpes – it was miserable and wet outside, which had put me in a wistful mood. My now ex-boyfriend put this song on the jukebox to keep me happy while he pumped endless coinage into a bandit machine. I was alone in a corner, a bit annoyed, when the music swarmed all over me. Filled with unfathomable woe I purposely dropped and smashed a glass of bitter. I saw the gesture then as symbolic of my melancholy: I know now it was merely a stupid, drunken stand against the mentality of the blonde-hungry males who frequent popular Rotherham night-spots. Unfortunately, my boyfriend failed to see it that way and promptly dumped me for being a crackpot mardy bitch.

GRAHAM COLEMAN of Hampstead, London

First heard on a Peel session in (correct me if I'm wrong) September '84. One afternoon at home in the summer holidays I was consumed by that kind of wrap-around blanket boredom which leads inexorably to self-disgust. I played this song over and over and decided drastic action was required to break my gloomy mood. I had been training for the football season and thought that some physical activity might help dispel the blues. So, despite the rainy conditions, I went for a run.

I ran for two hours that day, fuelled by a furious desire not to live out the self-pitying, defeatist lyrics of 'How Soon Is Now?', while clinging to them as a comforting echo of my condition. I got back, soaked to the skin, heart pounding, knees throbbing. And played the bloody song again.

KENT BURT of St John's, Newfoundland, Canada

Hatful of Hollow was the first Smiths album I owned. I bought it one day while out shopping with my parents. During the hour's drive home I read the lyrics over and over again, filled with a tremendous sense of exhilaration. Every song spoke directly to me – spoke *for* me. I was such a desperately lonely teenager. The last three years of high school were especially traumatic, for I was just then coming to terms with my homosexuality. I grew up in a tiny seaside town of some 200 people. It wasn't an easy place to be a little different, far less a little homosexual. Being both, I was doubly fucked.

All men have secrets and mine was bigger than most. Having no one around to talk to who might understand made me feel utterly alone. I firmly believe that if it were not for The Smiths, I might not be alive right now. This song, more than any other, was my comfort. Not because it said I was normal or anything, but because it reassured me I was not alone in feeling alone. There were others out there who felt my despair and the cause was unimportant. Normality wasn't just the issue. I didn't care if others branded me a 'freak' just as long as there were others who, like me, were 'waiting'. Like me, I guess they're waiting still . . .

ANDREW P. DAVIS of Aldershot, Hampshire

A Christmas party with the crowd from work. A torrid, stale affair full of the people you loathe during the day and carefully avoid at all other times. You stand with your drink, wondering why the hell you came. Was it out of choice or obligation? Then a special song fills the pub and you look around but no one else appears to have heard it or reacted to it. It fits this occasion perfectly; far more so than the sugar-sweet yuletide selection which will soon return.

Of course, the others don't want to hear it. A song all of my own – just for me. Happy Christmas! Sod the rest of them.

JO COOPER of Hampstead, London

I still smile at a fable regarding this track which emerged from the tour of Scotland in autumn '85. In order to perform 'How Soon Is Now?' live, Johnny had to pre-record the guitar 'whine' which is the song's hallmark and activate the tape by means of a foot pedal. The road crew, a bunch well known to The Smiths and other Manchester bands like New Order and The Fall, had other ideas.

At a convenient moment prior to the soundcheck, the recording was switched for one which bellowed 'Fuck off, fuck off, fuck off!' When Johnny hit the pedal, he was apparently *not* amused to hear the sound of echoing expletives bouncing off the walls of the venue.

HUGH RYCROFT of Oval, London

In August 1984 I was in Liverpool with my (by then) ex-girlfriend. She'd ended our affair a couple of months previously, but with spectacular foolishness we'd agreed to go ahead with a long-standing plan to attend the annual Beatles convention. The atmosphere between us was hellish – on her part, I perceived an unwillingness to communicate. God only knows what she identified on mine.

One evening, in a state of confused despair, I was sitting in the room flicking through local radio stations when I chanced upon the new Smiths single, 'William, It Was Really Nothing'.

This cheered me up somewhat. There followed another song, obviously by the same band, although I didn't know what it was called ('Please Please Please . . .', I would later learn). Incredibly, a third track of haunting beauty meandered its hypnotic way into the room. It talked of going home, crying and wanting to die. 'Yes,' I thought.

It finally finished, whereupon I was to make three discoveries. First, that I was tuned to Manchester's own Piccadilly Radio. Second, that these three brilliant songs could be found on one twelve-inch single, which seemed as commercially preposterous as it was artistically commendable. Third, that this band The Smiths were destined to mean more to me than The Beatles ever had. A defining moment indeed.

JAMIE BEEDEN of Cheltenham, Gloucestershire

Myself and Tommy had gone to a club and all night I kept seeing this beautiful girl wearing a Smiths T-shirt. She had lovely big green eyes and blonde hair and without difficulty I convinced myself that she was glancing more than occasionally in my direction. Fired with Dutch courage I decided to ask this wonderful woman to dance. I could hardly walk straight with nerves and the words seemed to stick in my teeth like chewing-gum. 'Er, would you like to er, er . . . dance?' I was almost apologising to this girl for daring to exist near her. Her friend nudged her and said something which might have been, 'Go on – he's not *that* awful', but alas, she refused and muttered something about a bad leg, and smiled an apologetic smile. I shrunk about three feet and grovelled away, crushed. Desperately trying to appear casual, I slunk off to the gents – there to be consoled by Tommy. In my despair I hear the opening bars of 'This Charming Man' coming from the dancefloor and we crash forth like two demented greyhounds. There she was. Dancing with some fella and showing no sign of being inconvenienced by leg injury.

At the close of the song she flashed this hulking behemoth a dazzling smile and they returned to the table. I started looking around for Tommy and couldn't believe it – he was in a deep snog with her friend! Everyone but me was doing it! At that, the restorative strains of 'How Soon Is Now?' enveloped me and I closed my eyes and laughed out loud and threw myself on to the dancefloor like a man possessed. Everyone else might disappoint me and ignore me but this band and these songs were MINE and at that moment they were all I wanted and all I needed.

NICK KING of Nottingham

The latter half of the eighties was the most miserable time on God's earth, particularly if you were a supporter of Notts County. At that time football was the only thing I had in life but for what seemed like an eternity we were stuck in that bloody Third Division. And so I'd be travelling on the train (alone, since everyone else supported Forest) to miserable grounds in places like Rotherham and Doncaster waiting and praying for promotion to brighten my dull existence. 'Well you say it's gonna happen now . . .' I'd stand on the terraces, as often as not watching my heroes lose, and then return to Nottingham just as everyone else was streaming into town for a Saturday night out – friends, couples, gangs and lovers. And I was going home to spend the night in, on my own.

SANDRA BANFIELD of Manotick, Canada

After being tricked once too often in bars, I can't enjoy this song until I'm sure it is, in fact, The Smiths and not 'Hippy-chick' by Soho. The track evokes a vivid memory of a vacation I took with fourteen friends in the Dominican Republic. One night we all went to a bar where the music was awful, so after plying the DJ with drinks all night he agreed to let us take over the booth to play the records we liked. When 'How Soon Is Now?' came on, I sang along – karaoke style – over the mike in my frighteningly tone-deaf wail. Fortunately, everyone else was equally drunk and incapable of remembering.

ADRIAN HOWARTH of Sale, Cheshire

She had gone on a college trip to Stratford-upon-Avon. How uncaring; my life was over! I couldn't eat, I couldn't sleep and, yes, my bedroom was filled with the smell of teen angst as I spent Bonfire Night alone with only candles for company. Is there really anything to live for? Yes, *Hatful of Hollow*, a bargain at five quid but more than that, a lifesaver.

On her return we had to go to the college Christmas bash in a nightclub. A proper jacket and shirt seemed to be in order and we set off, only to fall foul of the then ubiquitous 'no jeans' ruling. Walking home past the Arndale Centre, three townies took a dislike to us, grabbing my girlfriend's bum and punching me in the face several times. God, the shock. We stood in a phonebox and cried buckets. I'd never felt so low, and on my return home played 'How Soon Is Now?' over and over. It helped a lot. I recall the feeling of isolation. Me and Ian Curtis both.

CLIVE of Kingston, Surrey

Following twenty stifled years in the cloying bosom of the most insensitive family imaginable, I found a legitimate means of escape in the form of polytechnic. Any hope of change, however, was unfounded. After being cheated out of my childhood and teenage years, I had no idea how to form friendships and considered other people generally contemptuous if not hostile. I was reduced to a circuit of tacky pubs and worse clubs in the company of the 'mates' with whom I had the misfortune to share a flat. It was '87/'88 and The Smiths had come and gone, the backlash already setting in; although none of this was to my knowledge.

I was, however, intrigued by the subculture of people who looked really weird and had, apparently, more to live for. I resolved to 'get into' alternative music. Before long I was up to my ears in the output of various punk/gothic bands, conspicuously more offhand and politicised, but still none the wiser. Around this time I was contacting kindred souls on the database, one of whom recommended The Smiths. On this advice I purchased *Hatful of Hollow* (it being the cheapest album), and initially considered it a bit too lame to be 'alternative'. It grew on me, however, much aided and abetted by the stunning 'How Soon Is Now?'

Suddenly life took on a whole new complexion. More by luck than judgement, I'd stumbled across what I sought: a convincing antithesis to the attitude that non-compliance renders one an nth class citizen. That's bullshit – because it serves to further polarise the gulf between the emotional 'haves' and 'have-nots'. Class war. Battle was joined . . .

CALUM McGILP of Studland, Dorset

This track transports me back to the summer of '85. My sister and I were 'caretaking' a student friend's flat – feeding the pot plants and fat cat were high on our list of duties. The student's record collection was like a cellar of fine wines; never before had I enjoyed unrestricted access to such riches. Among my first, wide-eyed selections was *Hatful of Hollow*. This song opened my eyes . . .

CLIFF NORMAN of London, W9

Throughout my life, I have often been somewhat slow getting into things . . . Didn't pick up my first guitar until the age of nineteen, when most would already be playing in bands . . . Couldn't stand football until I attended my first match at fourteen and I've been hooked ever since. The story goes on. First sexual experience at the ripe old age of seventeen (last of the famous international virgins!). Consequently, and entirely predictably, I wasn't moved by The Smiths immediately. With so many fake and shameless bands around in the early eighties, my first, cynical, reaction was, 'The Smiths – probably yet another bunch of trendy student tossers.' As a result, four singles passed me by, with only 'What Difference Does It Make?' raising minimal interest.

My conversion was to come about in the back of a cold, draughty, uncomfortable Transit van headed back to London after a gig. At that time, I played bass in a nine-piece ska band called The Potato 5. Feeling drunk and low and in need of some stimulation, I little knew that the radio was about to provide some . . .

Into the van comes that haunting, distorted guitar followed by the crash of drums and bass. And then THAT voice singing THOSE lyrics which had been penned just for ME. Yet another late start.

JENNIFER BOARDMAN of Union Springs, New York, USA

Unlike the vast majority of eight-year-olds, I spent a great deal of time in my local cemetery – thinking, musing, playing with myself . . . normal stuff like that. One day, I came upon a dirty, slightly broken cassette tape. It was not pre-recorded and I had no clue as to what might be on it, if anything at all. I left the tape where I'd found it, and next day brought along a small recorder. The music started the moment I pressed the 'play' button. That single instant remains my most thrilling sexual experience to date. Whoever had done the recording had placed the song twice on each side. The cassette featured no other songs.

My exotic and treasured discovery was to last me four short months. So thin did I wear the tape that to my dismay it broke. I still had no idea of the song's title, or its artist or anything –

just that it had come to mean something very special to me. From then on I had to content myself with playing and re-playing it in my head where it was firmly lodged.

Five years passed before I heard my song again. I could hardly speak. This time I found out its title and artist. I was thirteen by then and fully ready to appreciate the brilliance of The Smiths.

STEVE KALINOWSKI of Bangor, Maine, USA

One of the first songs to grab my attention was 'How Soon Is Now?' Although outgoing and gregarious, I had always been a shy lad when it came to love and this song became almost an-themic to my desire to love and be loved. My abiding memory centres around a school dance in a neighbouring town attended by myself and my then girlfriend. This school could be relied upon to serve up better sounds at their dances than ours, and the DJ played this track before long. I was immediately grabbed by a girl from the host school who just wanted to dance to her favourite song, and it was fun to see the wicked glares being cast by my girlfriend, unaware of the special bond which exists between Smiths fans.

GIORGI KHABURZANIA of Tbilisi, Republic of Georgia

The day before I left Tbilisi, my home town, to study in Amer-ica, will all my life be connected with this song. That day my close friends came to say goodbye. I knew we should have said some special things, but we didn't. We were too sad. But what made me even more miserable was that the one I loved didn't come to say farewell. She didn't even call. It's not that I ex-pected her to show much attention towards my leaving, but I did kind of hope that at least she'd be there. But she wasn't and that was that.

When my friends left I felt very lonely and insecure so I just sat and listened to 'How Soon Is Now?' – the song I love to hear when I'm sad. Then I called my best friend Kaha and talked to him for several hours. I told him that after our conversation I would listen to this song, and he understood how I felt. That night I didn't sleep and early in the morning was at the airport with the song playing in my head. It represented that part of my life which I was about to leave behind.

Now I am in America for six months (six months is a long time) and whenever I write Kaha a letter, in the end it always goes, 'P.S. I still do listen to my song.' And really, I still do.

GRAEME LILLEY of Newark, Nottinghamshire

As an ardent moviegoer, the typical pre-film advertisement has always struck me as something of a cultural monolith. Each visit throws up the same old attempts to persuade audience members that their lives really cannot continue without visits to 'Chalkie's Tanning Palace' or 'Vindaloo Express'. The actors always look like they ought to be welded to a hostess trolley. If you've seen them once, you've seen them a hundred times . . . Or so I thought.

My then girlfriend had called from Leeds on the Friday afternoon with the news that an unexpected extension had been granted on an all-important politics essay and that this, she'd decided, would be her last weekend of concentrated debauchery before buckling down to some work at university. That I liked the sound of, and within an hour was climbing aboard a northbound coach armed with a six-pack of cheap Nordic lager and a tin of red paint.

Both were to prove inappropriate, for on arrival her visions of an expansive weekend had shrivelled somewhat to a movie-and-a-meal kind of evening. I groaned, but only inwardly, sensing that dissent might jeopardise any carnal bonus to come. Off we set. Queueing at the ticket booth, the ritual which must be familiar to all long-distance lovers was faithfully enacted.

Wallet open . . . and open to inspection. Followed by interrogation: 'Whose phone number is that?' 'Who's she?' The personal vetting didn't last long, which was good, but only because she'd spotted two tabs of extremely strong acid. And this was bad – much worse than unidentified phone numbers or inch-square photographs of unknown females. Unable to deny their presence, I went for the next best option – lie. 'Oh, they're tokens from Ribena cartons,' I said, adding for effect, 'I'm saving up for a blackcurrant watch.' Placated, if not fully satisfied, she made for the theatre doors. I don't know quite why I did what I did next, but I did it all the same. I popped both the Ribena tokens and followed her.

'. . . the authentic taste of Punjabi!'

'. . . Kwik Cabs – best prices in town!'

The ads are on and things are becoming a tad scrambled. I am struck by the sweeping grandiose melodrama of the Pearl and Dean music. Suddenly, I think I can hear the opening grind of 'How Soon Is Now?' But then I've just dropped two tabs of acid. It couldn't have been . . . How the hell can everybody be sitting around when the bloody Smiths are on?

Incensed and inspired, I began thrashing around – waving my arms in the air and singing. And there *are* no words: this is an ad for Pepe jeans. Heaven. Oblivion. A spiky mish-mash of sounds and images. The Smiths. 'There's a club if you'd like to go . . .'

A small man with a moustache tugs insistently at my arm. 'It's time to go son, let's be having you – no trouble here.' I turn for some support but an untouched coke and a packet of wine gums are the sole occupants of what had once been my girlfriend's seat. Quickly, dizzily out into the blistering cold, I grab the slowest cab, driven by the most dishonest cabbie in the world and spend a tenner getting back to her place.

The note was pinned to her door: 'Don't bother knocking or my brother will break your legs. The next bus is at 6 a.m. – take it and never come back. Count the seconds on your blackcurrant watch.' Game, set and match to her. A night in a freezing bus station, watching the drunks wrestle while on acid. And all thanks to The Smiths. Their music was just *too* good, the bastards.

GEMMA MALTBY of Brentwood, Essex

Apart from this being the story of my sad little life, several images immediately spring to mind: Sean Hughes prancing about thrusting daffodils into the air; Morrissey wannabes taking over the dancefloor and strutting their stuff with pained 'Oh I desperately need to be loved' facial expressions; the Capital FM DJ Neil Fox because he always uses the song as background music (but unfortunately never actually plays the whole thing) and above all, it is the ultimate voice sticking up for me against all those Cilla Black matchmaker types who think it is amusing to put me through the agony of being set up with somebody who I fancy the pants off but do not have the nerve to look straight in the face, let alone have a conversation with. If it was not for this song I would be feeling ten times more lonely than I do now.

CHRIS BAILEY of Wisbech, Cambridgeshire

After another dreaded, compulsory, muddy and, as usual, completely unsuccessful rugby match, the 'macho' fighting began all around me in the coach. I plugged in my headphones and, as the jock-straps and empty coke cans flew over my head, thanked God that there was one other sane voice on this bus.

LAURENCE HUGHES of Tufnell Park, London

I think it was around July 1985, and I was cycling along the east coast of the island of Mull, in the Hebrides, on a journey that took me many a weary mile through Harris and Lewis and

Skye, and back to the mainland. I had some kind of cheap personal stereo to keep me company along the way. I had already worked my way through my Orkney Strathspey and Reel Society tape, and was now listening to a cassette a friend had thoughtfully supplied me with, of selected Smiths tracks. I had been aware of The Smiths since the very first singles, but *this* was the moment it really hit me (the song was 'How Soon Is Now?') just *how* wonderful, just how refreshing for the tired and hungry soul, they were. So now part of me will be left for ever, bowling along in a stiffish breeze by the sparkling sea, singing at the top of my voice 'I am the son and the heir of nothing in particular . . .'

MARIAN COLE of Brooklyn, New York, USA

This song always articulated my seemingly endless wait for a lover, or even a boyfriend. Now that I've been initiated into the glories of sex (Ha! Morrissey was right all along about celibacy) it's still meaningful.

ALEXANDREA SEMINARA of Pennsylvania, USA

In 1986 I was at a sophomore high school dance when those first soul-stirring chords of 'How Soon Is Now?' came over the sound system. I had first heard of The Smiths only a few weeks before. A friend had made me a tape of her favourite Smiths songs which I listened to night and day on my cheap portable cassette deck. To hear this song clearly, its loudness reverberating off the gymnasium floor, thrilled me. This beautiful sound baffled them – were they to slow dance acned cheek to acned cheek? Breakdance? Most opted to sit on the bleachers and gawk at those of us who danced the way the music made us feel, not how the television told us how we should be dancing.

I found myself flailing my arms in the air, twisting and singing aloud in ecstasy. I felt so close to Morrissey and so far from the people around me. Every word from the song stuck in me like a sword of truth. That song at that moment gave me a realisation that shaped my youth. I *was* different. Everyone pointing and laughing at the dance already knew it; it just took this song for me to realise (and accept) it.

KHRIS TIMMONS of Greenock, Renfrewshire

1991 or '92. I arrived home from a bad night at Paisley Tec student union after enduring hours of shitty rave music and several knockbacks. It was around three as the kettle boiled and I began twiddling fairly aimlessly with the radio dial. Nothing but crap love songs to punctuate the spark and crackle. The last station was playing this song. Somebody out there knew how I was feeling.

STUART of Shepherds Bush, London

A Thursday night, February 1985.

At the tender age of thirteen the gentle strains of childhood's swansong have long faded as I take my first fumbling steps into the horror world of adolescence. *Top of the Pops*, always a weekly ritual, brought to my notice an awkward ungainly fellow singing beautiful verse and expressing feelings of sadness, inadequacy and regret, layered with a heartwrenching melody. I knew I had found friends, allies, a guide to lead me.

Believe me, love at first sight or not, this was no puppy love – this was the real thing.

ANDREW PARKINSON of Wimblington, Cambridgeshire

1985 – sitting, bored and listless in my room trying to revise for some dreary banking correspondence course. 'How Soon Is Now?' was getting quite a bit of radio airplay then, which was one mercy, I suppose.

KEITH WRIGHT of County Armagh, Northern Ireland

I remember standing at a urinal in a pub one night, arguing (if you could call it that) with a bloke. Both of us wearing Smiths T-shirts, his conviction was that Morrissey himself was The Smiths, while I felt (and feel) that the band were much much more than that. Dissidents should listen to 'How Soon Is Now?' and with that, I rest my case!

TOM BENHAM of Rochdale, Lancashire

I suppose the memory that will always return when I hear this song is when, as a rather bored eighteen year old, myself and a very close friend (who shall remain anonymous) used to take our parents' cars in the early hours of the morning and head up to Southport, where lies one of the last remaining beaches you can drive on. We would then spend the next couple of hours tearing up and down the beach racing similarly reckless youths in pursuit of momentary glory. Another favourite pastime was to drive as fast as we could around the mini roundabouts on the sea front until either we bottled out or the car span off. Now, these nocturnal trips were always accompanied by the same tape to be played in the car, the most memorable track of which was 'How Soon Is Now?' Not that it held any particular meaning to either of us, but if played very loud it was the perfect piece of music to accompany some manic driving.

I Keep Mine Hidden

TOM GALLAGHER of Giffnock, Glasgow

An odd song of scant appeal and little consequence, but one whose personal significance clings doggedly.

Few have been the Greenock Morton matches I have *not* attended, these last twenty years or so. As a youngster, I developed a coping ritual to see me through those isolated, nerve-shot Saturdays when illness or family holidays enforced my absence from the game. Determinedly ignoring wireless updates and even the teleprinter, I would wait instead until the 'official' classified results appeared on the Beeb read by that familiar voice to which no one can ever put a name. Kneeling within arms' length of the television, I watched much in the manner of any normal, well-adjusted person until the appearance of the page prior to that which would contain the life-affecting scoreline. This used to be the English Fourth Division, when Morton enjoyed a place among the elite of Scottish football. Then, just as the result from Wrexham or Workington or York City was being called, a large book or newspaper would be placed over the central column which would very soon display our number of goals for the afternoon. Thus a preview of the opposition's tally could be gained (0 or 1 auguring well) before whipping away the shield to reveal our true fortunes. The whole process was both comforting and enormously thrilling.

The other week, I had a pint with Andy Mullen in The

Tankard. Andy has a fiancée and a mortgage and a proper job. We got drunk and I confessed, at the age of 28, to still 'keeping mine hidden'. Andy considered awhile before passing judgement: 'You're as sad as fuck, Tam,' was his damning verdict. He's probably right, but then, Andy has never listened to The Smiths. For now, at any rate, I'm happy to keep on keeping mine hidden.

RALPH THOMPSON of Archway, London

For my sins, I studied for most of the mid-eighties at Dundee University. My parents, as most Scottish expatriates are prone to doing, fostered the romantic notion that somehow if I gained an education at a Scottish university then in some small way my grandparents' displeasure at their departure south would temporarily abate.

This was 1985, a year best remembered for the Bradford fire disaster, the Heysel tragedy and the Sinclair C5 fiasco. For myself and undoubtedly thousands of like-minded others, it was a time of restless, reckless and thoroughly wasteful behaviour set against the ugly backdrop of flyaway popular tunes by Nik Kershaw, Billy Ocean and (surprise, surprise) Madonna.

That summer, that hollow beast which laughingly calls itself the music industry was, in my opinion, singularly to blame for a variety of misdemeanours perpetrated *en masse* by the youth of our area. On one particular, admittedly beer-fuelled, August evening, I can recall a massive fracas breaking out in the local pub as a direct result of my mate Eddy taking umbrage at a selection made on the jukebox. He didn't like 'Obsession' by Animotion and decided to let the poor girl who selected it know all about it. Much to her obvious chagrin, Ed deposited a squashed, half-eaten Mars bar in her drink. She turned around from the jukebox to be met with the sight of this pissed halfwit hoisting up his trousers with a grin like a prize-winning marrow grower. Ed disappeared into the sweaty mass of bodies and made good his escape. Unfortunately, the girl noticed that the rest of us were in knots laughing at this bizarre scene and vented her justifiable anger by throwing both glass and contents in our general direction. She may have had the girth and strength of Ian Botham but if Beefy had been this off-target I think he may well have been paid a visit by the local branch of the Drugs Constabulary.

Needless to say, all hell broke loose. To cut a very long story short, the ensuing trashing of the pub was the talk of the town and, suspecting my involvement, my parents insisted that I pulled myself together et cetera. Unbeknown to me, plans were already afoot to hasten my departure. It became evident that much maternal weeping and gnashing of teeth had been met with an equal amount of grandmaternal weeping and gnashing of dentures. The game was up and I was packed off to Dundee to take up a place on a course at a university whose letter of acceptance I had no intention of even doing the courtesy of rejecting.

Gradually, I settled into this grey, grim city. I still smile when I think of the proliferation of 'disco-pubs' which the 1980s threw up all over the country. For a guy who had had to leave home as a result of one of these lifeless dens, I seemed to spend an inordinate amount of time in them. But then, anything is better than actually attending classes when you're a student. Many of my fellow students clearly felt the same way as no matter what time of day one entered the pub there was a 99.9 per cent chance that there would be someone to share your acerbic view of life as an impoverished scholar. The chat would, more often than not, turn to football and the alternate fortunes of my team, Arsenal and usually Dundee or Dundee United.

As most denizens do, I found that I had established more than a passing interest in the more successful of the two teams – United. I became a token 'Arab', the nickname adopted by the United fans, and as such opened up a whole new social world to myself. A couple of guys from the uni had offered to take me to the next home game and with a newfound zest for life I hungrily agreed.

Where, you must be wondering, do The Smiths fit into all this? Well, the story goes something like this. I had been a fan since day one. Everywhere I went The Smiths came too. For a while I even tried unsuccessfully to look like Johnny. It's not too easy when you're seventeen stone. Undeterred by my portly gait, I would faithfully try to copy the great man Marr's fashion sensibility. Unfortunately I tended to end up looking more like Captain Birdseye for some unknown reason. Anyway, bedecked in this quasi-nautical garb I set off for Tannadice with high hopes for a good day out and hopefully, a good night into the bargain. The game was disappointingly awful. United were trounced. After the second goal went in Paul, one of my escorts for the day, turned to me and said, 'I wish I was happy in the haze of a drunken hour,' to which my immediate reply was, '. . . 'cos heaven knows we're miserable . . .' '. . . in front of goal,' interjected Danny, to much laughter. From that moment on, any chance for Smithsular banter was instantly seized upon. This tradition carries on to this day. In May of 1994 when United beat the mighty Glasgow Rangers to win the Scottish Cup I received a phone call from the lads, drunk on the team's victory (and some Scottish lager no doubt), chanting from a phonebox one of my old favourites. 'Orange and black, a stumbling block, we've an eleven man defence, which you cannot unlock . . .' I could almost smell the Bovril.

I Know It's Over

NICK KING of Nottingham

Even though I loathed school, I dreaded the day it would end for I knew that would signal the abrogation of my pious hopes for a relationship with the classmate I so adored. That day finally came in June 1986, and coincided with the release of *The Queen is Dead*.

For me, this song was just so bloody poignant. About a week later I watched from my window as they walked hand in hand and I knew that it was, indeed, all over. What had, in truth, never really begun.

To the refrain, 'Oh mother ...', I opened my diary and wrote, 'Today I died inside – my life is now over.' Self-fulfilling prophesy or not, it still rings true these many years on.

JENNIFER BRUNDAGE of San Jose, USA

This song was absolutely crucial to my becoming a fanatical devotee of the band. I was going out with a person who, it was becoming increasingly obvious, was not very deep. He was attractive in certain ways but I could never get over his saying flippantly, 'I just don't understand people who mope about the past – it's just not important.' This was (is) so at odds with how I felt that I knew our views would never correspond. For a time,

I grudgingly tolerated his finding Dinosaur Jnr superior to The Smiths (big of me, eh?) but one night, alone, listening to 'I Know It's Over' I took the words to heart and we never spoke again.

RUSS C. S. THOMAS of Ferndale, South Wales

This song is extra special – who could possibly get over lost love without it? My thoughts were reaffirmed recently at a drunken party in Blackpool, of all places. I enjoyed a long, pissed-up chat with Keren Woodward of pop-dollies Bananarama. She told me how she'd virtually lived with this song after the break-up of a long relationship, and of how the 'Nanas were desperate to cover a Smiths song ('Sheila Take A Bow' I reckoned!). Keren went on to tell me of drunken London nights with Johnny Marr and of Johnny's rather excellent take-off of Beverley, Alison Steadman's horrendous 1970s creation from *Abigail's Party*. Apparently, his recorded messages on the answerphone would often feature 'Bevspeak'. I was stunned and impressed by Keren's total knowledge of The Smiths – Bananarama, of all people, were desperately in love with Morrissey.

CHRIS NANOS of Toronto, Canada

I can listen to the live version from *Rank* over and over again. I don't know – it's just so beautifully written. It's almost as if you have to listen to it when you're alone which is sad, I guess.

What kills me is that I know there are people all over the place listening to this song on their own. Frustrated, depressed, tired, lonely. And I know I'm one of those people. It kills me that we all have something in common and we'd get along for sure if only we got together. But we don't. There's too much bullshit which we don't deal with or can't deal with or won't deal with. Maybe we don't know how and we certainly don't know why. Whatever.

All Men Have Secrets

MELANIE NEWMAN of Brentwood, Essex

A girl has a phone conversation with a boy she's never met. They unfold their lives and over a period of weeks get to know one another inside-out. Over the next couple of months they fall in love, amazed by the feelings they experience and one day they meet. It's awkward and neither feels quite the way they did before. For the girl, it intensifies, while for the boy the feelings diminish. They meet a few more times until finally the boy stops calling and refuses to answer the phone. The girl doesn't understand what's happened – she's tearing her hair out with worry, believing he still loves her. After all, he'd said it so many times.

They finally speak one morning before she goes to work and he tells her he doesn't love her anymore. There seems no particular reason for this. He just doesn't.

This song seems to be about myself and this boy. 'It's over, but it never really began.' More often than not, the reality doesn't fit the dream.

CLIVE of Kingston, Surrey

No – I've never got on very well with the opposite sex. I find the whole idea of cattle markets, chat-up lines and dates (all in an atmosphere of cut-throat competition) entirely repulsive. That said, I still experience emotional need, so what do I do? There's nothing much I can do – except think and dwell and get very depressed.

Why must a conversation degenerate into a battle of wits almost every time? Does no one else respect sensitivity? And if they did, would they look for it and even value it in preference to the easy option? Probably not . . .

To try to help someone is to risk feeling guilty and what an acute taboo that has become, of late. So often I feel like nothing as I climb into an empty bed. Perfection! Nobody ever expressed it so accurately. '. . . But in my heart it was so real.' How many girls' answering machines have I left that on? I lose count!

ANDREW TAYLOR of Bootle, Liverpool

Summer 1986, again – the eve of a trip to Belgium with my friend Nel to stay with relatives in the improbably-named town of Leper. My parents had gone off on holiday themselves and the house was littered with notes written in Mum's familiar hand: 'Make sure the boiler is off', 'Make sure the bins are empty', etc., etc. Contrary to their belief, I wasn't really alone in the house at all, since most of my friends had moved in just as soon as Dad's car disappeared down Rainbow Drive. My girlfriend, Ruth, was then touring Europe with a friend and a backpack, and despite my houseguests I felt slightly lonely and fearful of the future. This song was played over and over in an attempt to make me feel closer to her.

The odd thing was that our paths were due to cross in Belgium in less than three weeks' time, and knowing this tempered the sadness of the track and acted as the spur for a great holiday.

BILLY EVANS of Basingstoke, Hampshire

Bang, bang, bang; goal, goal, goal. Ten minutes played and our dreams of cup glory are shattered for another season. Fucking manager – should stick to headmastering. We're all out of position! I've never played left-back in my life and to cap it all, there's Dad and his bloody mate hugging the touchline in their bloody awful sports jackets. 'Yeah, Dad, I know – it's not about winning.' Blah blah fucking blah. It's always the same. He turns out once every hundred years and we're utterly cursed for a full 90 minutes.

And just what was the idea of making Peters captain? Dad thinks he's great of course ('Born to lead, young Peters') and will never accept that he's the biggest wanker in the school. Nice girlfriend, though – bastard. She introduced me to The Smiths during a school trip to France in third year, shortly before convention gripped her by the lapels and transformed her into a very stuck-up head girl. Never forgave her for selling out. Wanted to but just couldn't ... Foul, free kick, goal, four. Shite.

MARCO BILYK of Basingstoke, Hampshire

For all its melancholy and morbidity, I love this song. One that I played after being dumped by a girlfriend in 1992 and which is a sad reminder of a turbulent ending to a strange relationship. When Morrissey sings 'I know it's over and it never really began/ But in my heart it was so real' it sums up that whole episode in a nutshell from her saying, 'I think we should finish,' the walk home trying to convince myself that it was probably for the best and then the dawning regret and realisation that I had let slip someone special. 'I Know It's Over' is a theme tune to a relationship taken for granted because it began at the wrong time ...

JONATHAN WALSH of New York, USA

At the risk of being damned by legions of The Faithful, it always struck me that The Smiths' forte was that of simple communication; in short, the lyrics. Alone in the shower, the songs sound best not whistled but sung. In a way matched only perhaps by Billy Bragg, lyrics are the body and soul of each track – instrumentation rarely dominating in the way it does for, say, The Stone Roses. It was surely no coincidence that Morrissey cut his teeth at a time when Sid Vicious and Wolfgang Iser were shaking the world of musical perception by its collar, if not quite shaking the world.

With so much at stake in each Smiths song, they are apt to become, for the attentive listener, more Proustian Madeleine than three-minute diversion. Perhaps tellingly, the recollections which bubble into the mind's eye are, more often than not, those nostalgic and melancholy memories of a not-too-distant past and the too-real present. Albeit arriving late to the ranks of The Faithful, I have been moved by every track in some way, by some more than others, and by 'I Know It's Over' more than any.

I confess to having difficulty with relationships, and should really avoid them as does a prudent hare the hounds. Yet, with a seasonal regularity which recalls the migration of geese, I find myself promising the world to yet another thinly-veiled wolf. That tired equation's sole variable lies in how the wolf will choose to dispose of me. The variations have been endless – all of them good and valid and painful beyond words.

The most recent was played out against that most romantic of backdrops, the train station. It was a typical Manhattan December – cold and dark between the powerfully illuminated buildings of town. I walked away from a woman I had not intended to love, but had all the same. She found another, and our attempt at 'talking things through' had proved an exercise in chilly futility, walking cold streets for an hour or more. I remember only the steam from roasted chestnut stands and the taste of too-salty pretzels. Although alone, now, for the first time in a year, I was glad to be among the rush and push of the city. Distractions presented themselves as if in consolation; queueing for Knicks tickets to give Father for Christmas and humming along with a Salvation Army choir.

It was not until I met my sister at our suburban train-stop that the impact of what had transpired was able to claw its way into my comprehension. Waves of hurt; her final line: 'Never lose your smile and never forget me for I shall never forget you.'

Finally, I was alone, climbing into bed, reaching for the arm of the record player, falling into the darkness. 'If you're so funny, then why are you on your own tonight?'

SARATH SAN of Cergy, France

I was spending two weeks in London during my parents' divorce. In fact, I wanted to forget 22 fairly messy years and think instead of a new start. One afternoon, I was listening to my favourite Smiths songs – of which this has always been one. How can I describe this particular moment? I can only say that it was an odd, though very comforting sensation to feel every word and sound as though it was my very own creation. My soul was marked. I felt my simple truth.

Is It Really So Strange?

JAMES CALLOW of Ulverston, Cumbria

The lines of this, one of my favourite tracks, never fail to make me think of a local road sign which reads, 'The North – Carlisle/The South – Lancaster.' Small world?

JILL PRESTON of Burnley, Lancashire

We were in a club in Corfu and so drunk that we didn't even think it really so strange that this was played. Me and Sue were inter-railing and had met a couple of Irish lads. They were brothers and we'd got talking on the ferry over from Brindisi. Once in Corfu, we'd got apartments next to each other and had spent the week drinking and smoking dubious Irish substances.

It was as this record came on that Phil announced, in a slurred voice, that he could consume no more alcohol and was going to bed. He staggered off and we returned to our drinks.

It might have been a few seconds or a few minutes later that we heard the shattering of glass in the distance. Someone had walked through the glass door of the club on their way out. Once again, we returned to our drinks.

At around four, having lost Bertie in some dark corner of the club, Sue and I wound our way back to the apartments. Passing Phil's door, which was open, we decided to look in on him.

'Have either of you any idea how I did this?' he asked, in his now familiar Irish lilt, as we entered the room to find him prostrate on the bed, covered in blood and one of his legs gaping open.

It was one of those moments when the only appropriate thing to do is laugh. The hospital could wait for a few minutes. Amidst the blood and drunken confusion we laughed and laughed. Until, that is, Sue fainted, slid down the wall and landed in a crumpled heap on the floor.

A strange night indeed.

I Want The One I Can't Have

TRACEY HOLLOWAY of Bristol, Avon

1984 to 1986 were important Smiths years for me. I was then studying the history of modern art, design and film at Newcastle Polytechnic. I was into everything from Dirk Bogarde to radical feminism when along came the Bequiffed One. Songs like 'Handsome Devil' and 'I Want The One I Can't Have' fuelled my obsession for a fellow student initialled MW. My feelings were not reciprocated; she was obsessed with Malcolm, our shambling tutor!

'Just meet me in the alley by the railway station,' I crooned tunelessly to a backdrop of anti-Thatcher demos, *The Godfather* and teacakes. 1985 grew increasingly depressing as I struggled to cope with final exams, a confession and ultimate rejection by the object of my admiration. I did, however, see The Smiths twice that year at Newcastle and Bristol – perhaps this saved me!

Facing a bleak future, what did I do? Attempt suicide . . . ? Plan a high-powered business career . . . ? No, nothing so extreme. I simply joined the Labour Party, got involved with the militant tendency and cheered the Liverpool councillor Derek Hatton at the Royal Albert Hall.

Before long, I met Dave and thought, 'Hooray! My time has come at last.' But Morrissey, damn him, reared his lovely head again. Dave was celibate, and fond of quoting lyrics which endorsed his stance – 'I could have been wild and I could have been free, but nature played this trick on me' – from 'Pretty Girls Make Graves'. He then exited stage left, with my copy of 'Hand In Glove'.

KENT BURT of St John's, Newfoundland, Canada

The title alone endears this song to me. Ineptitude aside, as a gay man I've encountered a lot of oppression and bigotry. A former roommate of mine once opined that 'all fags should be rounded up on an island and blown up'. I got out of that situation pretty quickly. The first line of this song is for him, and all those like him.

I Won't Share You

ZOE of Victoria Park, Manchester

We were strolling through the Burton's Arcade in Manchester one chilly spring afternoon in 1991 when we spotted the busker. Shivering, he stood outside C&A strumming tunelessly; he seemed like any other busker. He must have spotted my Smiths T-shirt, however, for as we passed he began to play 'Cemetry Gates'. My friend and I stopped in our tracks and rushed over to him, giggling and throwing pound coins into his guitar case. Clearly, he was delighted to see us, not simply for the money but for the company. People to talk to.

It transpired he was unemployed and could fathom no other way of getting his rent money together. There followed a lengthy discussion concerning The Smiths, New Order, Morrissey concerts, the merits of Electronic and whether Morrissey would ever reform the band. Sadly, our train-time was approaching and my friend and I had to rush off. Our parting exchanges were a bag of Maltesers which he attacked with grateful gusto and from him, strict instructions to listen to the B-side of *Strangeways* . . . The album in its entirety wasn't (and isn't) one of my favourites, but 'I Won't Share You' is a beautiful song and one which will always remind me of him. We'd discussed our favourite tracks and it was in his all-time Smiths top three.

I'm sure I saw him once more, buying copious quantities of

books in W. H. Smith. I'd love to think it was him and that better times had come his way. Or maybe there were simply lots of Smiths T-shirts around that year.

DEREK LENNON of Glasgow, G12

Sitting in a crumpled mess in the corner of my bedroom listening to *Strangeways* . . . Thinking about her and what might have been and the regret and anxiety becoming too great to cope with. Then, before I can torture myself any further, this comes on – screaming around the room with heartwrenching beauty. I want to cry over the loss of someone very special, but instead I smile for a moment and forget her.

NEIL McNAB of Islington, London

The posthumous release of *Strangeways* . . . came at a time which was as grim for me as it was for Britain's greatest band. Knowing that the album represented the last batch of new songs I would ever hear, and not wanting them to be forever associated with such a dismal phase of my life, I decided to put the whole LP into mothballs. There it would remain, unplayed and unheard until happier times when the prized tracks could be savoured to the fullest.

Of course, a few songs were aired as singles or were memorably performed by Morrissey early on in his solo career. Those who I told of my pledge generally respected it, even if they did question my sanity. One exception took place during a tipsy night in Marylebone when a friend insisted on my listening to her cherished 'I Won't Share You'. Nevertheless, the album in its entirety remained an unknown quantity until one fateful summer's day in 1990.

I had joined a coach trip visiting 'Smiths Landmarks' in and around hallowed Manchester. It was hot and sticky; the ennui only partially relieved by Smiths songs being played in between the tour guide's cheerless commentary. Unalert, I distractedly hummed along until to my horror, the unfamiliar strains of something which could only be one thing drifted from the loud-speakers. Powerless to escape, within minutes and in the most infelicitous cicumstances my noble abstinence had been broken.

With hindsight, perhaps serendipity was at work, for *Strangeways* . . . was to become my very favourite Smiths album. But alas, nothing now remains to be uncorked years on, like a fine wine. All the songs, in all their glory and with all their qualities, are inextricably grounded in the band's and my past. Yet oddly, my regret is tempered by the nagging feeling (cynics might call it wishful thinking) that, ironically, *Strangeways* . . . may yet prove not to have been the last word after all . . .

Jeane

IAN GOLDSACK of Maltby, South Yorkshire

Always a favourite, I really came to appreciate this song when living out at university. I'd sit at my desk, stomach rumbling, staring out at the gravestone works which backed on to our tiny terraced house. And I was Jeane. Yet I knew there was a way out – I was still young. But what of those whose long lives are spent in grimy, dead-end streets like that? Theirs are lives of monotony and monstrous despair.

STUART DAVIS of Haywards Heath, Sussex

Sitting on an Intercity train from Leeds to London last autumn, an attractive woman of 40ish caught my eye and smiled warmly. 'Jeane' was playing on my walkman at the time. Instantly, she became Jeane and it was as if I was singing the song to her in my head. Sadly, she got off at the next stop (Doncaster) and we didn't speak. Despite this, I was intrigued and fascinated and will always be reminded of her when I hear this song.

MELINDA HSU of Fresno, California, USA

I always figured Jeane to be a woman. Sometimes I thought of her as the mistress of the splenetic Charles Baudelaire. Her name was Jeanne, and it's quite possible to imagine Baudelaire venting the selfsame sentiments at her.

JOOLZ SMYTHE of Kentish Town, London

Prior to hearing this song, I imagined the title to be pronounced Jee-ann but that's hardly relevant to the story. After hearing this song, my fey notions of bedsit glamour vanished, and that *is*.

I once signed up for a series of nightclasses at a local community centre entitled 'Car Maintenance For Beginners'. At the time I didn't even own a car but figured it would be handy to know just a little about them in anticipation of picking up an old banger sometime soon. The course, of eight, hour-long sessions cost only £40 which seemed pretty good at the time. Predictably, the class of twenty-odd compromised a mixture of boy racers salivating at the prospect of bored-out cylinders and retirees in sports jackets intent on squeezing a few more weary miles from their 1968 Austin Cambridges.

The girl in the checked shirt with dark curly hair arrived on the second Tuesday evening. Her name wasn't Jeane, it was Polly, and by class four I was in love with more than just the guaranteed lift home in her little red hatchback. Polly loved The Smiths (especially Mike) and my fair-to-middling knowledge of the band was sufficient to make friends in the first instance, and to guard against awkward silences in the few weeks thereafter.

Polly lived in a bedsit – I, then, still with my parents and I must confess to have felt more than a twinge of inadequacy in this regard. Her habit was to drop me some five minutes' walk from home which suited both of us. Actually, it didn't suit both of us at all, because at least one of us had spent the previous fifteen minutes praying for red lights to prolong a journey which was becoming ever more intoxicating with each passing week. But as the classes wore on and we learned of points and plugs, neither the invitation to carry on home with her nor the mention of a date seemed to occur.

By week eight, I was convinced that my feelings for Polly were being returned. We had become, if nothing else, really good friends although the stilted atmosphere in the car that night belied this. Why the hell were we talking about the bloody nightclass when every bright green light sneered the dribbling away of a friendship? Because *tonight* we couldn't say, 'See you next Tuesday then?' That's why. Tonight would either say something substantially different or say nothing at all save goodbye.

Who said what doesn't really matter, I suppose – and in any case it was stuttered in a most uncool way. Not the kind of transcript I'd like to see in black and white. But the upshot was I did get to see Polly's bedsit – a tiny, cold, peeling attic which smelled of fresh paint that was nowhere in evidence. We kissed as 'Jeane' played, beside her laundry basket and an old pot plant whose earth had spilled on to the threadbare carpet.

RACHEL CROOKES of Cosby, Leicester

I am wholly convinced that this track nods in the direction of Shelagh Delaney's *A Taste of Honey* – the tale of a semi-whore and her daughter imprisoned by the grime of industrial Manchester. Of course, the play has been plugged plenty by Morrissey and has even been cited as the reason why The Smiths wrote like they did.

That's as maybe, but 'the low life has lost its appeal' strikes me as being an alternative phrasing of 'poor is beautiful'. Jeane is me, I am Jeane: I too walk the streets and find them cold and teeming with false promise. I once believed the song to contain the line, 'I don't believe in marriage anymore.' It seems to fit rather well.

Last Night I Dreamt That Somebody Loved Me

GRAHAM COLEMAN of Hampstead, London

The intro to this song always brings to mind *A Tale of Two Cities* which is really strange since I've never read the book. I believe the main character is beheaded in the end and maybe the sounds evoke a group of people gathering for an execution, chattering in the sunshine while they await the grisly entertainment.

It's the strangest feeling waking up after dreaming of one's ideal/mythical partner and being jolted back to reality by the sense of loss – which lingers and haunts you throughout the day. You know all too well that in real life you'll never love someone that purely. Real arms around you are a different kettle of fish. That distressing chasm between illusion and reality. Sitting in a cold room in Cricklewood waiting, just WAITING for something to happen to me. 'The story is old, but it goes on . . .'

It's so UNABASHED. There's no layer of irony or protective cynicism. That's often a recipe for disaster, but they got away with it – time after time.

HOWARD TINKER of Crewe, Cheshire

I remember the summer of 1987 like it was yesterday; twirling joyously around my bedroom, imaginary gladioli clutched to my chest, dancing with unashamed abandon to the strains of 'Sheila Take A Bow'.

The Smiths were the band who launched a thousand quiffs and made a nation's youth glad to wear glasses. Steven, Adam and myself were eighteen, clumsy and shy. We found even ordering a pot of tea a tortuous ordeal. The Smiths were our band. Their appearances on *Top of the Pops* became events of unparalleled importance and the release of a new single meant a nervous journey home, lest I be knocked over on the way – tragically doomed never to play the record.

At college, we spent countless hours discussing the finer points of Smithology and fell to conversing in Smiths quotes: 'Let's give up education as a bad mistake.' We had found a language for our misery.

Marooned in the Alan Bennett zone of Southport, we desperately craved glamour and excitement. Instead, pot-bellied lager louts brawled on the promenade and coach parties of senior citizens marauded shamelessly across the sands.

That summer I left college, finding myself dazed, stunned, on the dole and uncertain of the future, but strangely content. As The Smiths soundtrack played on, I gloried in youthful apathy and teenage ennui. Idleness was turned into an art form – something to be prized and nurtured like a prize tomato. And yet something was missing. A gnawing void. Until one day I realised what it was.

A quiff.

I longed for my hair to be like Morrissey's, and resolved to cultivate an enormous bouffant worthy of my status as a card-carrying Smiths devotee. Now the seeds of teenage rebellion were well and truly sown. Builders barracked me, neighbours crossed the street to avoid me. My lust for vengeance was satisfied.

We spent that summer wandering aimlessly around the sleepy seaside town; its seafront shelters, its shopping arcades, its second-hand bookstores and its coffee shops. Ours was a *Boy's Own* world of Smithdom, a female-free zone where girls seldom ventured. For the most part, we were far too cowardly to have wanted it otherwise. We consoled ourselves with the fact that at least it kept things uncomplicated. Everything in the garden was pretty rosy, but of course that wouldn't last.

One day The Smiths split up. I read about it in the *NME*. Within days, depression set in like arthritis. Idly, I considered the possibility of running a hot bath, climbing in and cutting my wrists with my mother's Bic razor. I decided against it, choosing masturbation instead. In a cruel and meaningless world, self abuse offers a young man hearty solace.

The posthumous release of *Strangeways* . . . coincided with my meeting Adam one last time before he left for university. Afterwards I lay on my bed with arms outstretched as if crucified, and listened to the album with religious reverence. 'Last Night I Dreamt That Somebody Loved Me' seemed to articulate the glorious misery of my impoverished existence. It put the tin hat on things nicely; tormented soul shrieking above pounding piano as that swirling James Bond theme thunders in and Morrissey wails, 'The story is old, but it goes on . . .'

Eventually, inevitably, all three of us would escape the cloying grasp of that dreary coastal town. But that album and this song in particular will forever evoke a strange time. My years as a teenage vegetable. Youthful yearnings and tearoom dramas. When every coffee shop waitress held the promise of illicit liaisons and an invitation to sexual adventure could be distinguished in the clink of a tea cup.

GAYE HUTCHINSON of Maltby, South Yorks

The night after I'd first heard this song is one I'll cherish forever. I actually had a dream that Morrissey, wearing a brown woolly jumper, embraced me in his arms then took me flying. It was dusk, and as we floated serenely over my home town of Maltby he would whisper in my ear points of interest to be seen from the air. I vividly recall him saying, 'Look, Gaye – there goes a tree.' OK, so Maltby isn't exactly overendowed with interesting landmarks, but that dream remains poignantly special as a reminder of the night Morrissey loved me . . .

STEVE KALINOWSKI of Bangor, Maine, USA

October of 1987; eighteen years old and I get to learn yet another of life's harsh lessons. That it hurts to be used. I had taken a week's holiday from work to fly down to Washington D.C. to see some friends prior to enlisting in the army. Most unexpectedly, I got hooked up with an old flame from some years before. We shared a rather intimate evening and the next day she insisted on throwing me a farewell party. I guess the previous night must've meant more to me than to her, because she ignored me for most of the do supposedly held in my 'honour'.

It was late by the time everyone headed off and I found myself lumbered with the clearing up duties. She went upstairs with some bloke who was friendly with her ex-husband. Rather than sit around listening to the mattress squeak, I left and spent the night sitting on a porch eating chocolate-covered raisins and getting very drunk on vodka and peach soda. I had recently purchased *Strangeways* . . . and played this song so many times that eventually the tape broke part-way through.

Ms NICK BURTON of Braunstone Town, Leicester

I relate this one to football because of the crowd SFX introduction and also because my team, Leicester City, have endured such dreadful luck at Wembley. (One win in seven attempts since 1949.) Definitely the intellectual 'You'll Never Walk Alone'!

NORMAN CUMMINS of Govan, Glasgow

This song always brings back memories of a New Year party held in my house in '91. Myself and four friends had all brought copies of *Strangeways* ... and by three in the morning were pissed out of our heads, sick to death of Trivial Pursuit and singing along with drunken gusto. This song really hit the spot and was requested several times. It was interesting that the people who once slagged The Smiths now bought their albums.

ALEX GREEN of Uddingston, Lanarkshire

'No hope, no harm – just another false alarm.' Wee Coke sat alone in the corner, the smile draining from his face as the tears coursed down his cheeks. Hard times had come to the Smiths Aficionados' hacienda. Wee Coke was just the latest. Big Chic (just back from America where he'd had to leave his sweetheart), Wullie Bowman (perennially unlucky in love), and myself (marriage over, thank God, but left feeling like a failure) were sitting trying to console ourselves when the spurt of blood flew over the coffee table. The wee man had taken one of his darts and sliced it across his arm. We sat rigid; shocked. Then he stood up and said, 'I fuckin' love that song – now who's getting me an ambulance?' Wullie began laughing, shock and nerves setting in. By this time the wee man was covered in blood.

We waited at the hospital while Coke's arm was stitched up. After signing himself out, we got ourselves a quarter of the local shrubbery, a few bottles of wine and set off home again. We listened to The Smiths for the remainder of the night, chatting, laughing and even then beginning to make sense of everything. 'The story is old, but it goes on ...'

ANGIE J. LEWIS of Huddersfield, Yorkshire

I can remember being on a bus one day in 1989, returning home from yet another tedious day at work (I was a VDU operator, and worked with CDs which was my job's one saving grace) listening to *Strangeways* ... on my walkman. I got to 'Last Night

. . .' and felt totally in despair as I listened to Morrissey's pitiful and anguished lyrics. I knew exactly what he had gone through (and probably still is) because I was experiencing the very same. I'd never had anyone ever at the time, and I really didn't think I ever would. I saw my reflection in the bus window, and I immediately wanted to throw myself off and lie down and *die*, because what I saw frightened me almost to death. I was looking at a face that was desperately sad, eyes that had never known happiness. 'Last Night . . .' epitomised the deep depression I couldn't shake off, the loneliness I knew I would inevitably suffer until the day I died . . . I'm a little older now, and although I've had boyfriends and everything, I'm *still* entirely lonely and I'm *still* waiting . . .

London

TOM HALL of Southgate, London

Aged sixteen and clumsy and shy, I was beginning to get itchy feet after five years at Bishop Douglass school in East Finchley. The setting itself didn't help, being a dull, grimy and wholly uninspiring suburb of north London. My only escape route seemed to be the local sixth form college and even that offered little by way of a change, far less the excitement I sought. Another factor in the equation was Jennette Maciejczek, with whom I'd been secretly in love for years. She was beautiful and nice, but steadfastly if politely ignored my Smiths tapes.

On the morning of my last exam, I was walking as usual through the screaming horde of first years when 'London' came through my headphones and drowned everything out. Morrissey was saying, 'Go on – what have you got to lose?' I took the plunge that day and walked out after the exam, intent on never returning. And when saying goodbye, in the eyes of some who were staying I *did* see resentment. I can still picture the vile sixties buildings disappearing from view on the bus home as Johnny's heavy riff kicked in. Just one example of that voice in the corner of the bedroom pushing me on to different places, different times.

All Men Have Secrets

JOE REEVES of London

I grew up in a backwater of Reading, the grey, dismal town that most people only pass through on the train. Whenever I could, I would travel up to London (you would never travel 'down' from Reading) to amble along the King's Road or work my way through the racks of winklepickers in Kensington Market. I'd always go by bus to escape the wretched Reading shoppers queueing up with their pink nylon pillow-cases and brown slip-on shoes as if there was nothing better. The bus was cheaper than the train and somehow more satisfying as we ploughed our way through the passers-by on the High Street. I'd slip on my headphones, The Smiths blasting into my ears, and look out on the rain-spattered people who remained oblivious to where I was heading, the fact that I was leaving, albeit for a day.

The Smiths' 'London' summed it up. I couldn't wait for the moment when I could go. Really go. The moment that I could look back at my home town and feel pity for the people still there with their little lives and their small concerns. 'You think they're sad because you're leaving/But didn't you see the jealousy in the eyes/Of the ones who had to stay behind' sang Morrissey into my head as the safe houses, the two-up two-down square semis with mown lawns, were replaced by the leering, concrete towers of Hammersmith. Eleven years on, now settled a few miles from those west London towers and asphalt flyovers that first greeted me, I return to my home town filled with the same loathing, Morrissey's words as contemptuously important as ever. It may have turned out to be as grey and dismal here, there may still be shoppers picking over pink nylon pillow-cases, but I've made it. I've escaped. I made the right decision.

Meat Is Murder

SHELLEY HODGSON of Harold Hill, Essex

My most illicit 'liaison' to date occurred only months after I'd discovered the true grandeur of The Smiths. So proud was I of my latest (and greatest) acquisition, *Meat is Murder*, that I decided it would provide the ideal musical accompaniment to an evening of amorous endeavour. Fearful of that dreaded moment when passion's height coincides with the end of the record, I placed the disc on never-ending 'shuffle' facility and set about the business in hand with the gusto which an easy mind brings.

True to form, the album *did* provide a most pleasing and atmospheric backdrop to the proceedings. Having bought it only hours beforehand, however, I was yet to become fully acquainted with the heartrending melodrama that is track nine. I can only conclude that fate's cruel hand was shuffling the tracks that night, for as previously uncharted peaks of ecstasy were ascended, we became aware of the sound of distressed bleating and mooing in the background. As a confirmed vegetarian, I am slightly abashed to admit that on this one occasion I was rendered helpless by uncontrollable fits of giggling. Morrissey – the passion killer . . .

GILAD CARMEL of Tel Aviv, Israel

The lyrics are out of this life, and the addition of the cattle sounds makes me *feel* like the butcher. I'm not a vegetarian, and

113

probably never will be, but still this song makes me think that man is a predator.

ANGIE J. LEWIS of Huddersfield, Yorkshire

I remember eating some chicken (or something equally repugnant) directly before playing the entire *Meat is Murder* album, which I'd bought after an 'exciting' day at work. At that time I was employed as a VDU operator at my local council which was Kirklees Metropolitan. I was 'honoured' to have the task of word processing the results of meetings of the schools in the area, such as minutes and agendas. Enthralling stuff or what? Anyway, I felt quite uncomfortable and guilty eating that chicken, because the title said it all. So when I got to the title track (I was at home in Huddersfield on an October night in 1988, listening to my walkman yet again) I braced myself for the punishment that Morrissey would mete out for my wretched sin of eating some unfortunate creature. And what I heard put me off meat for life. The lines 'The meat in your mouth as you savour the flavour of murder' especially hit home, and I knew from that moment that I would never eat meat again. And do you know something? I haven't.

Miserable Lie

SALLY of Bristol, Avon

Around the time of the debut album I fell in love for the first time – with an incredible boy named Skreet. Much as I loved him in my own pointless manner, I was a shit. Most sixteen-year-old girls are, I suppose. After a time I felt remorse at 'destroying his flower-like life not once but twice' (actually, it was more than that), and decided to send him some flowers. I went to the Interflora shop and asked what they could do for me. The minimum order, it transpired, was six quid – around half of that would have assuaged my conscience nicely. After ploughing through the book of arrangements and finding that six quid didn't go very far, I decided to send Skreet the balance in gladioli. The spray concealed an awful message about how I promised not to do his head in anymore. I did see him a few more times. I don't know how many gladioli £6 bought in 1984, but he reckoned his house was full of them.

KIM DAVIS of Loveland, Colorado, USA

Loveland? Terrible little place! Honestly. No one has ever heard of The Smiths and not a single soul knows the first thing about taste or style. I don't doubt that most of them believe Europe to be a coffee parlour somewhere in London. The name is the only charming or unusual thing about the place . . . a bit like Whalley Range. Thank you, Morrissey, for knowing exactly what I'm talking about.

MALCOLM GREEN of London, NW6

It was the winter of 1983, living in a squat in West Hampstead, leading an anarchist-activist lifestyle. All vegetarianism, Crass and running squat clubs. The Smiths had been raved about by the *NME* for some time, but had never played London.

When it was finally announced, their first capital appearance was as support to Howard Devoto at the Lyceum. I think the bloody awful Sisters Of Mercy were also on the bill, but my memory obviously refused to take in any information about them. The Smiths fumbled on to the stage amid a wash of dry ice. They looked decidedly weedy, Johnny Marr in particular – it was probably the big hair and huge guitar strapped across his almost man-size chest.

They sounded dreadful. The guitars whined and the rhythm section were almost anorexic. Morrissey swooned and posed, waving his flowers around, looking for all the world like a young Larry Grayson on LSD.

My first thoughts were that this lot were just another puny white indie hope destined to fail with the first album. The black leather and mohican-clad audience listened quietly to begin with, and then, as this song started, they all began laughing, heckling and jeering. The bars filled up.

And suddenly, I thought, 'Hang on, there's a song here.' They were so unlike anything else around at the time. The dance scene was just beginning, The Clash had discovered hip-hop, the pop charts were full of synth-pop and here was a band who sounded like Roger McGuinn fooling around with Nick Drake's younger, camp brother.

The set didn't get much better, but the hatred with which the band had been received by the rest of the crowd made me want to like them. So I did.

Money Changes Everything

LITO MARTINOU of Athens, Greece

I first heard this song back in 1987 when the special, Greek-only limited edition EP was released over here. It featured five tracks: 'Bigmouth . . .', 'Panic', 'The Draize Train', 'Unloveable', and 'Money Changes Everything'. I was only a thirteen-year-old girl at that time, but The Smiths had already become the ones for me – a position they still, and will always, hold.

So, after I bought this treasured EP I brought it home, placed it carefully on the turntable and sat down to enjoy it. Halfway through the B-side I realised that one of the tracks was obviously missing something. 'Money Changes Everything' had no lyrics, a lousy title and – yet – a wonderful tune. I quickly decided to take matters into my own hands by providing the lyrics myself! After around a dozen plays, the words began to flow and took the form of a hastily written poem. Over the next couple of days I worked on them until I felt ready to record a 'complete' version of the track with myself filling in for Morrissey!

I do not wish to sound big-headed, but it remained my favourite track until Johnny decided to have another go and it became 'The Right Stuff'. However, the tape with my very own, alternative version is safely tucked away, in a drawer in my room – protected, like all secrets ought to be.

All Men Have Secrets

PETE of Broadstairs, Kent

Money can change everything. It took me two weeks to save up for my first Smiths album and I've never looked back.

Never Had No One Ever

MARIAN COLE of Brooklyn, New York, USA

I could write a whole book about *The Queen is Dead*, which was released during my first week at university. It brings back every one of the emotions I experienced at that time of leaving home – excitement, fear, loneliness and all the rest. The lines in this song, 'I had a really bad dread/It lasted twenty years, seven months and twenty-seven days,' still sends a chill down my spine. I was twenty years, *five* months and twenty-seven days old when I first left home. Close enough, you'll agree, to be regarded as conclusive proof that Morrissey really was singing my life!

JON SCOTT of Putney, London

I cannot hear this song without being back there, on stage, the heat of the spotlights on my ears, entering and filling my head, catalysing my heart. I was playing a suave, unflinching gentleman in a play by J. B. Priestley, in a modern 'progressive' production at university, and this was the play's recurring theme song. All was going well. It was the final night and we were all looking forward to the cast party. We weren't just going through the motions, we were surfing on a wave of past hard work, rehearsals, arguments and fear; all was now beneath us, buoying us up, speeding us to shore.

And then I see her, then him. Cuddling in the second row, contentment in their faces, spite in their eyes. But I don't forget my lines. I am submerged in a furnace of hate, the second row (bitch) is only five yards away. I want to hit him and her, him the invader, the opportunist, her the deceiver, the ex. She looks lovely. Yet I carry on my role, say all my lines, forced smiles, unending pauses. It can't last. Morrissey comes in on cue, gradually, powerfully, soothingly, detracting from my presence, forcing me into darkness. I will never forget coming off stage to that song. It's silly how at the time it seemed so wise, so far beyond anything in the second row. The words meant nothing, but the whole song was poetry, way beyond the large clutching hands of her new boyfriend, impervious to her slight floral dress. The voice tailed away of its own accord: it was the end of our performance. I bow, swivelling my eyes from ground to clock at the back of the hall, straining to see the time. Party starts at ten.

Nowhere Fast

MARY DAVIS of Margate, Kent

Shortly before my eleventh birthday, The Smiths came to Margate. None of my friends showed any interest in going (they were all into Wham! at the time), and so I was forced to take my bossy sister who, at 27, would sooner have stayed at home listening to Gilbert O'Sullivan.

I think it was a Tuesday night but the date was definitely 8 March 1985. The gig began with 'Nowhere Fast'. I was stuck on the balcony with a bunch of stiffs. How I wanted to be downstairs, even if the crowd there were much older and bigger than me. Refusing to be intimidated, I waited until Big Sister was suitably distracted and sneaked off. My hand-me-down red anorak and M&S children's jeans must've looked strange among the crowd of *Meat is Murder* T-shirts, but I really didn't care.

It must all have been a bit like Moses parting the waves, because during 'How Soon Is Now?' I found myself only two rows from the front. An as yet unrivalled experience. Of course I was grounded on returning home, since for most of the evening Big Sister hadn't been watching me, but it was worth it!

CRAIG SOWERBY of Coquitlam, Canada

This is another song with great lyrics and great guitar. It's probably the best song for jumping around and singing along to. On a more sombre note, 'I think about life and I think about death and neither one particularly appeals to me,' is a fabulous line that describes how I feel sometimes. I may be bored with life but I certainly don't want to be dead. I think that line really sums up how apathetic one can get about life.

JOANNE CLEGG of Stockton, Cleveland

I had never experienced such cold in my life. It must have been November or December. We'd been to see James play in Liverpool and me and two friends were staying with Jonny, another friend, who was a student there. Jonny hadn't gone to the gig with us. When we rolled out of the student union, drunk and hot, we were suddenly enveloped in thick, freezing fog. We could hardly see where we were going, but headed towards the main road to get a bus or taxi back to Jonny's. By the time we got to the main road, we couldn't see each other, and there wasn't a car on the road. It was strangely silent, except for the odd high-pitched voice or distant laugh, but they could have been coming from anywhere. It was only now we realised that we had absolutely no idea how to get to Jonny's and that Jonny didn't have a phone.

It took us three hours to get back, stumbling blindly round the streets of Liverpool, almost hysterical, our lips so frozen we could hardly speak. If it hadn't been for a man leaving a pub, hours after closing-time, who literally bumped into us and then took pity on us, I'm not sure we would ever have found the right road.

Jonny was still awake when we got back. He was in bed, smoking. My friends slept in his flatmate's room, who was away for the night, and I crept into Jonny's bed with him. *Meat is Murder* was playing, and as I dragged on his cigarette, still shaking with cold, 'Nowhere Fast' came on. Never had the title of a song been so apt. Never had I been so grateful to be inside: in this bare, stark, damp room, with its 'Hand In Glove' poster clinging to the wall by one corner.

Paint A Vulgar Picture

MARY DAVIS of Margate, Kent

When *Strangeways* . . . was released and I first heard this song, my mother had just started work at a tiny independent recording company. Just how tiny it was is illustrated by the fact that it specialised in what I called 'Catholic Exotica': taped religious music and lectures and all manner of stuff. I was intrigued by the whole scenario. At the same time my first band were coming to a rather acrimonious end. Our drummer (who owned all the gear), wanted to play 'Pump Up The Jam', I wanted to play 'I Am The Walrus' and our vocalist seemed fairly indifferent to the prospect of playing at all, preferring horse-riding to rehearsing. This song's depiction of the darker side of the music industry rang so true, even though I was involved in what amounted to little more than the tiniest microcosm of it.

I myself now work at the 'Catholic Exotica' stable – and can report with pleasure that everyone and everything there seems perfectly honourable and upstanding!

IAIN KEY of Cheadle, Cheshire

Did WEA fail to spot the irony, or was Moz playing on his Ouija board?

All Men Have Secrets

CLARE GOUDY of Brighton, Sussex

Curiously enough, a potent reminder of the time I painted my bedroom during the summer following my GCSEs. At that time, The Smiths were relatively unfamiliar (I had just bought *Strangeways . . .*) and this song seemed to sum up the burgeoning relationship I was enjoying with my new heroes. I spent the best part of two weeks holed up in my room trying desperately not to splash the skirting boards and feeling a tremendous rush of pride each time I heard the opening riff. At last, a band worthy of adoration! I don't remember much else about that summer, save for the nagging (and totally unfounded) fear that I might have botched up my exams. I suppose that's why this song has come to mean so much to me; it's my sixteenth summer squeezed into five minutes.

Panic

ROB MARSHALL of Wood Green, London

Another day dawns at the General Dental Council (for it is here I waste away, daily) and not even a dream laced with Shelagh Delaney kisses can lift my flagging spirits from the well of apathy into which they plunged many decades ago. The word processor blinks threateningly, awaiting a further bout of verb and vowel acrobatics, but the language it speaks renders my already chilled heart cold. A pile of letters from Swedish dentists lies on my polished desk demanding answers, but I care not – as the milkmaid of Whalley Range once remarked, 'It says nothing to me about my life.'

COLIN SHORROCK of Chorley, Lancashire

During those school-torn years of 1982 to 1987, my sole interest in life was the blue and white halved shirt of Blackburn Rovers FC. I lived and breathed football – read *Fever Pitch* by Nick Hornby and you'll get the idea. This, of course, was the time that Messrs Morrissey and Marr were tearing the music world apart and causing uproar in teenage bedrooms the civilised world over. All this passed me by – no *Hatful of Hollow*, no quiff, no *NME* or Salford Lads Club. *The South Bank Show* went unwatched, I knew nothing of The Smiths and music was of scant concern. Just *Sports Report* of a Saturday evening and Ewood Park . . .

One Monday morning in 1988 all this was to change. I discovered The Smiths courtesy of the Radio One Breakfast Show. An unlikely source indeed! 'Panic' was played, the first song I'd really listened to and certainly the first to engage my attention. Suddenly music became an interest, or the music of one band at any rate. Tapes were borrowed (*Rank* being the first) and before long I was to buy the first piece of vinyl I'd ever owned – *Hatful of Hollow*. At last, football had a rival suitor for my affections.

So I'd missed The Smiths, the interviews and concert tours, the hype and television appearances, but Morrissey was then striking out on his own and I resolved to be there every step of the way. Without that initial hearing of 'Panic' I'd never have queued for seven hours outside a Manchester record store, and I wouldn't have taken to the road in February '94 to follow Morrissey's tour. That song was my introduction to music and life, and represents a debt I shall never repay. Spare the DJ!

MILLIE RUST of Hammersmith, London

Hanging around London on hot summer nights with friends.

STUART DAVIS of Haywards Heath, Sussex

Some time ago, I was lead singer and rhythm guitarist with a Leeds-based four-piece named Backwater. In March '93 we were in the process of recording our first demo. Prior to setting off for the studio one morning, I decided to 'psyche' myself up by listening to 'Panic' by The Smiths. It had a strange and over-powering effect on me (if not the desired one!) and the words and music refused to leave my head.

During breaks in recording I would pick up a guitar and sing and play the song repeatedly. This did not endear me to the rest of the band. I even resorted to covering some posters with the lyrics.

When finished, that demo sounded really good. Inspiration!

STEPHEN KING of Clarkston, Glasgow

My story recalls that celebrated period of a young man's life during which we drink ourselves sick of a Saturday night while still being able to claim half-fare on the last bus home. For myself and the rest of the post-school/pre-adult infantry which would make its goggle-eyed way into the city centre, a path to Strathclyde University's student union was invariably beaten in haste.

Our choice of venue owed much to the near-legendary lenience of the union bouncers – a clueless and motley assortment of ex-hardmen native to the Lanarkshire hinterland. For them, weeding out fresh-faced seventeen year olds from beardless eighteen year olds was evidently about as appealing as learning to recite the Koran in nine languages. We passed without let or hindrance.

Having been squeezed for the obligatory two quid admission, we'd make for the sweaty heights of 'Level Eight' by means of the ancient and rattling elevators. These, as I recall, were either hurtling earthbound at an incredible rate or stoically defying even the most frenzied bouts of button-pushing. Having secured one to ourselves, the night really began in earnest. About eight of us would stand stork-like on one leg, arms a-flailing, intoning the opening chimes of 'Panic'.

Seven floors of wriggling and jostling later, the cry would go up, 'Last one down's a Morrissey.' Panic in the lifts of Glasgow. As the lift juddered to a threatening halt, most of us would be thrown around mercilessly in our mobile iron dungeon. Someone, however, would always manage the impossible and contrive to remain upright, waving and singing and smiling. Morrissey for the evening.

It's both curious and comforting to reflect that the last one down is STILL a Morrissey – one Steven Patrick to be exact.

EDDIE PARSLEY of Kidlington, Oxfordshire

It's thought that Morrissey refers to Steve Wright in this song. He should visit Oxford and listen awhile to our local radio station – Fox FM. It's vile. All the instantly accessible (and eminently disposable) pop pap from four decades. I try hard to avoid it, but this is nigh-on impossible. Our only other local option is provided by BBC Radio Oxford – aimed squarely, it seems, at old codgers. A bit like Radio Two.

Distressingly, we now have bus services in the town which broadcast these stations through internal speakers. My purchase of my sister's old Metro around the time of this innovation owed nothing to coincidence. On taking delivery, I discovered three Fox FM stickers goading me from the back window. So stubbornly did they adhere to the glass that my efforts at scraping soon had to be abandoned. It surprises me enormously that Oxford's suicide rate is not considerably higher, what with the pressure of exams and Fox FM pumping out its aural sewage daily. The students either love it, or should be awarded firsts in silent stoicism.

Fox FM's mascot is Freddie, a kind of Basil Brush without the intellectual stature. I don't agree with blood sports, but reckon it's high time they set the hounds on Freddie. Tally-ho!

JULIE BALFOUR of London, N1

I always thought that the strongest bond imaginable would be between two supporters of the same football team. Of course, I was to be proved wrong! A couple of years back, I got chatting to a bloke from Manchester the night before the final of the fizzy-pop (a.k.a. Rumbelow's) Cup. It was soon established that we both were fans of Manchester Utd. Because of my non-Manc accent, he seemed intent on questioning my credentials as a Red Devil (footie fans are incredibly snobby that way) and suggested that I should be rooting for Arsenal, my local team. Despite showing him my season ticket for Old Trafford and telling him of my lifelong devotion to The Reds, he remained steadfastly unimpressed.

After a while the subject shifted from football to music and we got to talking of The Smiths. Common ground! His animosity towards me vanished without trace and when, by complete coincidence, the DJ played 'Panic' I leapt up and implored him to dance. In that peculiar Mancunian way he looked at me before saying, 'Oh, fuckin' 'ell – all right then.'

Later we made a haphazard arrangement to meet at Wembley the following afternoon, which was never kept. But the lads did win!

JOE GOODDEN of Bath, Avon

Scene: a city nightclub. Two hundred people revel in the sweaty atmosphere; kissing, drinking, but mostly dancing. The music thunders through the building like a benevolent dictator, while they gleefully celebrate the hold it has upon them.

One youth stands alone in the shadows, becoming increasingly disaffected. He picks us his coat, ready to leave. As he does, a new song emerges, its opening notes ringing out like chimes from heaven. He listens, awestruck, as the melody unwinds. Its uncanny freshness makes it hard to believe that the song is already seven years old.

And those lyrics! Bigmouth strikes, and every word that he says rings true: 'Burn down the disco/Hang the blessed DJ/Because the music that they constantly play/It says nothing to me about my life.'

It was the beginning of a beautiful friendship.

And I walk home alone. But the senses being filled are mine.

Please Please Please Let Me Get What I Want

TRAVIS GRAVELL of Smyrna, Georgia

Three weeks before Christmas '86 my father took me to a local record store. This particular chain, 'Turtles', generally stocked only ordinary domestic material. To my immense surprise, this store had a copy of *Hatful of Hollow* on cassette. After begging my father to purchase the tape for me, he agreed. On the way home I talked him into letting me have the gift early, and playing it on the car stereo. When we got to this, the very last song, I asked him to listen intently since it was my favourite.

Even now, I regard that tape as the most important gift I ever received. The gold rings, the bracelets and even the money have never meant quite so much. I've always wanted to tell my father about the significance of that simple gift, but have always felt awkward about doing so. Perhaps this way he can just read it.

EDD TRAVERS of Kirkintilloch, Nr Glasgow

When I stepped out into the bright June sunlight from the darkness of the assembly hall I had only one thing on my mind – what the hell was I going to do with the rest of my life? It was my final day at school and we'd just listened to the headmaster's speech wishing us good luck and safe passage in the world of college courses and jobs. Well, I was yet to apply for any jobs but knew for sure that my part-time hours in a local off licence would not (could not!) evolve into anything more permanent.

I recall trudging home filled with despair and anxiety. All around me, happy, excited, optimistic classmates babbled of grand schemes and career plans and summer parties to which I was not invited. I felt pretty hopeless and worthless and wholly bereft of any sense of belonging.

I got home and put 'Please Please Please . . .' on; I was to play this song an awful lot, actually, and I suppose it became my anthem that summer. It helped me to cope, if you know what I mean.

CHARLOTTE HALL of Leith, Edinburgh

One summer, I worked in a grimy, grisly pizza emporium in Glasgow – easily the most hateful job I've ever done. One of the chefs was a fervent heavy metal fan who played lead guitar in a band called Beast – name changed to protect the innocent! He fell inexplicably in love with me and displayed this affection by showering me with extravagant gifts such as Marillion tapes and anchovies straight from the can. Needless to say, he professed to hate The Smiths. I met him one day in St Enoch's Square and gave him my walkman to listen to the tape. The last song was 'Please Please Please . . .' Afterwards, he sat in silence and just looked at me. He loved the song, but never did get what he wanted.

ANGIE J. LEWIS of Huddersfield, Yorkshire

I always feel a tinge of sadness whenever I play 'Please . . .' because I'm reluctantly reminded of the (relatively) difficult life I've had. I more or less started fighting from the moment I was born, and have had to ever since merely to get anywhere in life. I don't know why, but I never seem to have had a lot of luck.

A lot of things were an obstacle to my establishing myself as a person (working-class immigrant background which is nothing to be ashamed of but, in this country, is not very helpful). But when I first heard 'Please . . .' (Huddersfield, at home, in October of 1988) it meant a lot to me to know that *somebody* out there knew what I was going through, and that they understood. When you feel as though everything is stacked against you (which I certainly used to) it really helps to know that you're not alone in feeling that way. Morrissey could have been reading my mind when he wrote those words, because they're so accurate it's frightening. I can only hope that those of us who are so very destitute will one day get what we want.

ANDREW PARKINSON of Wimblington, Cambridgeshire

Used, of course, as part of the soundtrack to the film *Pretty in Pink*. I love the scene where one of the characters sits alone in his room thinking of a girl and all the while tossing playing cards casually into a hat on the floor. The song seems to sum this up perfectly – definitely a 'chicken and egg' scenario.

PAULA CROFT of Skipton, Yorkshire

By some strange, lateral connection this song remains my own, personal soundtrack to a television series which was shown around the time the band were sweeping all before them. *One Summer*, as I recall, told the story of two Liverpudlian teenagers who, fleeing the police and a rival gang, hightail it to rural Wales and anonymity. There they found bed, board, friendship and a measure of guidance from a hermit-type who had beaten a similar retreat to a remote farmstead. Inevitably and distressingly, the trio's rural idyll was ill-fated from the start and collapsed around them in a welter of suspicion, betrayal and summary justice. I recall being totally absorbed by the series and its five or so episodes became required watching on Sunday nights – just as The Smiths were then prescribed listening for most of the other 167 hours of the week.

For me, the song 'Please Please Please . . .' articulated perfectly that burning desire for something better, something different. It seemed to mirror the boys' rather desperate, if noble, dream. I should love to see *One Summer* again (please please please, TV companies!) and shall be playing this song as they board a train bound for nowhere except away.

AMANDA of Pinner, Middlesex

I was fifteen, inexperienced and going out with Gaz. I'd met Gaz on holiday in Blackpool; he was older than me, wore a lot of black and drank a massive amount. We'd only seen each other a few times since we'd met (he lived miles away from me) so the question of sex hadn't become an issue, although I suspected it soon would.

This particular night we were at a party in Leeds and I found myself in a bedroom with Gaz. Somehow I sensed that he was about to address the subject but instead he walked over to the record player in the corner of the room, found *Hatful of Hollow* and played 'Please Please Please Let Me Get What I Want'. Lord knows it would have been the first time but, nice try as it was, he never did get what he wanted.

Pretty Girls Make Graves

ALEXANDRA HINCKS of Bath, Avon

God knows how, but we find ourselves in a gay bikers' pub – all Guns 'N' Roses and Jack Daniels. Suffice to say that the jukebox was pretty limited musically. My money clinks into the slot. Silence. I feel eyes burning into the back of my head, surveying my Smiths T-shirt and the gladioli-infested pocket of my jeans. Three plays later and I'm out of small change, but to ask for more would be courting disaster . . . in the car-park they're already preparing a grave and my name's on the tombstone . . .

MYRON PICKENS IV of Austin, Texas, USA

My appreciation of Morrissey's lyrics goes back to my secondary school days in Jakarta, Indonesia. For the spring break of '91, I went to the island of Bali, a popular location favoured by the 'ordinary' people. There, pub crawls and simple sex abound, and I learned plenty about the tangled web of life.

On my last night, I slept on the beach at Legion, Kuta with The Smiths debut album playing. Late night, slum street. Phrases like 'I've lost my faith in womanhood' might have been penned in this crazy, confused place.

RACHEL CROOKES of Cosby, Leicester

'I could've been wild and I could've been free/But nature played this trick on me . . .' was the line we back-bedroom casualties had been waiting for. Pugnacious!

MALCOLM GREEN of London, NW6

Mad Madelaine was beautiful. Small, dark, with a wicked grin and small scar above her left eye from a dog attack when she was four. We lived without hot water in a house surrounded by scaffolding which overlooked the canal. Jack the dog lived with us. We spent summer days walking on Primrose Hill with Jack chasing anything on four legs, or lounging on the scaffolding reading Sartre and Camus, listening to tapes through the huge cracks that split all four sides of the house. It was about five feet from the Euston to Manchester mainline.

At night we both drank far too much and mixed it with pills and acid. Poor Madelaine was never too stable when she was sober, and all we'd do was argue. But when drunk we'd fuck and fight and fuck again and it was great. Both stoned, listening to Tom Waits or The Smiths, it was love and lust but we never made plans. The furthest forward we'd dream was to the next Big Thursday when the dole cheque arrived and we could drink until midnight at The Lansdowne along with various Pogues and Big Olly the barman.

On warm summer evenings we'd dance around the living-room to 'This Charming Man' and 'Reel Around The Fountain' and at night, tossing and turning in the heat, we often fell out of bed twice.

By the summer's end Madelaine was gone. I came home to find Jack sitting on the scaffolding and a note pinned to the bed-room door. It simply read 'Pretty Girls Make Graves'.

She'd heard about me and Mary, a tall, willowy blonde with long legs and perfect skin.

I never saw Madelaine again. I heard that she married a

painter who lived in Chichester, had a kid and then left with the kid to join some travellers in Somerset.

Mary and I split up after three months. She didn't like the cracks in the walls.

The Queen Is Dead

GRAHAM COLEMAN of Hampstead, London

Take me back to dear old Blighty ... At a party in New Jersey in May '88 we, being the 'English contingent', were playing this song by way of a welcoming fanfare. It felt like we were being scrutinised – how would we behave upon hearing *our* music under alien conditions? Perhaps our hosts expected us to undergo some kind of atavistic reaction, grab the nearest spray of flowers and flounce around limp wristedly to amuse the natives.

Things did not improve. Later, we were all but force-fed an endless succession of lethal cocktails and asked to explain why the English are a race of savage football hooligans.

KENT BURT of St John's, Newfoundland, Canada

The other kids in school had barely heard of REM, so choosing The Smiths to analyse in literature class was perhaps a little perverse of me. But the bastards deserved it! No one had a clue as to the meaning of the song, least of all the teacher, although they did fare slightly better with 'The Headmaster Ritual'. Considering the subjective nature of 'meaning', there should have been 25 different analyses from the class – especially given Morrissey's lyrics. Alas, there was only mine, but that cheered me up no end. On the face of it, this song should hold little relevance for me since I'm mercifully remote from the tyranny of the royal family. That said, 'love, law, poverty' (and castration!) are all things that kill me, and my life has seemed longer than most. It's shortening now – thank God.

ELIZABETH GRIFFITHS of Toxteth, Liverpool

I possess a rarely-heard alternative version of this song. Instead of the familiar 'Take me back to dear old Blighty . . .' intro, it begins, 'Liz, you're not putting The Smiths on again are you? Liz, ARE YOU . . . ? Liz, please don't put The Smiths on again.' The accidentally-recorded pleading of a work colleague who'd simply taken too much.

ROB MARSHALL of Wood Green, London

It seems likely that my love affair with The Smiths began before I was even born. Had not the young Marr sought out Morrissey to insist on a collaboration, I would probably have invented them anyway. The words, seemingly borne of absolute physical necessity and tugging at the straps of so many cultural straitjackets left me paralysed. *Hatful of Hollow* left me shivering and wanting to do something anarchic like wading into the sea up to my knees. (As luck would have it the tide was out, but the thought counted none the less.)

And later, when *The Queen is Dead* arrived from the butcher's shop window, I set fire to Wigan Pier. No longer tormented by the pain of Samantha Smith's rejection, I cared not that five weeks' worth of homework lay untouched under the bed. My life was explained and exposited, full-stops, commas et al., within the green gatefold which housed what I still consider to be the finest moment of all. In those heady days, The Smiths were as vital to me as the air I breathed.

HOWARD TINKER of Crewe, Cheshire

It's sunny outside and I'm sitting in my room listening to *The Queen is Dead*. I've lived in this house for what seems like an eternity and more. Actually, it's been seventeen years. Kevin Marshall, my best friend from schooldays, has come round so I play him the album. We huddle round the stereo like boys round a campfire. This is an important moment for me because the world divided itself into two factions: the people who like The Smiths and those who don't. There is no in-between. Thankfully, Kev seems mightily impressed and when the record finishes he asks me to play it again.

And again. We study the album's sleeve, the insert, the gatefold. The photograph of the band outside the Salford Lads Club. It seems strange and mysterious and somehow other-worldly. Idly, we wonder where the club actually is, and what it's all supposed to mean. We play the album again and through the ritualistic process a childhood friendship cements itself in the adult world.

Things change. Years later, I bump into Kev while thumbing disdainfully through the *NME* in W. H. Smith. Different hairstyles, different clothes, different lives . . . The old house where I used to live has long since been knocked down. 'Do you still like Morrissey?', he asks, and the years roll away. At Christmas, we go to the Manchester Apollo gig, my personal highlight of which is a spellbinding 'Jack The Ripper'. Driving home on the motorway, Kev points out a small, undistinguished building at the end of a row of terraced houses. It's the Salford Lads Club. My thoughts wander to the day I first played him *The Queen is Dead* and I wonder if he remembers it, too. I say nothing, but know that somehow a circle has been completed.

HUGH RYCROFT of Oval, London

I spent part of the summer of 1986 working on an archaeological dig on the North Yorkshire moors. Along with a few professional archaeologists, there were about twenty of us volunteers, all living out of tents and sharing one cold tap and a particularly unpleasant chemical toilet.

In the face of such adversity, an amazing camaraderie grew up. We were a diverse crowd – a few punks, a few students, a woman taking a break from her husband, a crazy wandering middle-aged Spaniard – and the only common denominator was that we all seemed to have pitched up on this confounded dig in order to escape from something.

The Smiths were playing all the time, especially their new album, *The Queen is Dead*. In this outpost of squalor, so remote from the comforts (but also the rules, anxieties and neuroses) of normal life, the title track summed up the prevailing mood of newfound psychological liberation. Morrissey's bizarre and colourful fantasy served as our rallying cry. 'Her very lowness with her head in a sling' seemed like the ultimate escapist dream. It was easy to stick two fingers up to the rest of society and do what the hell we wanted for a change. We all seized the opportunity to go a bit mad, dyeing our hair ludicrous colours, and forgetting about the trivialities of personal hygiene and the like.

The memories linger of a happy time, some interesting and nice people, and one person in particular, with whom things never worked out quite as I'd hoped, but who will always remain extra special.

You don't like people just because they like The Smiths; but if they *do* like The Smiths, there's a fair chance they'll be of a similar mindset, and that seems like a pretty good place to start.

LISA JOHNSTON of Sweet Briar, Virginia, USA

My favourite of all Smiths albums. The title track is wonderful. It was also a tape a dear friend and I took to Finland with us on a crazy, snowy trip in March '87. We spent daytimes driving round and round Helsinki blasting this and nights dancing to it in gay bars. The Finnish friends we made loved The Smiths, but the country as a whole struck us as being very serious and melancholy. The city was plastered with posters hailing the release of a new collection entitled *The World Won't Listen* which we got upon our return to the States as *Louder Than Bombs*. It was also on that trip that I heard The Smiths on the radio for the very first time – Knoxville wasn't, and still isn't the most progressive of places, although the university station was beginning to cotton on to the band around then.

JENNY PARKIN of Huddersfield, West Yorkshire

Sunny Sunday afternoons, waking up in the banana-yellow bedroom of a second-floor flat. The room had a nasty block-mounted portrait of Steven Patrick on the wall – a bad pencil drawing, the sort men sell on the street, alongside cuddly dolphins, muscly men holding babies and Bob Marley smoking a huge joint. The bedroom had sloping walls and dormer windows, and if you stood on the bed and leaned out, you could see the whole village and fields beyond. A similar window in the kitchen was useful for ejecting all household rubbish on to the roof. The nights were beery, with the only decent CD in the house, *The Queen is Dead*, always stuck on continuous play by mistake. I would drift in and out of consciousness during those long nights and catch snatches of 'Vicar In A Tutu', or 'Cemetry Gates'. The housekeeper was a bit crap – a fat lad who really liked The Cure. He had a picture of Robert Smith on his front door, and a glossy book about them in the toilet.

DEREK LENNON of Glasgow, G12

The long summer of '92 and the music press, having long since exhausted the commercial possibilities of the 'Kill Uncle' tour, had focused its attention instead on Morrissey's alleged racism. My own conviction was, and is, that the dates at both

Glastonbury and Finsbury Park ought never to have been coun-
tenanced, far less accepted. Why stand among men envious of
your talent and ignorant of your genius?

Angry and bored, I travelled with friends to see James and
PiL at Alton Towers – Mike Joyce's appearance with the latter
acting as the main spur. Unfortunately, a terrific set by PiL was
delivered to a largely unappreciative crowd. John Lydon looked
distracted, while Mike seemed oddly sad. I was sitting on a
friend's shoulders when they returned for an encore which had
been solicited by only a very few. I shouted to Mike, and he
stared at me for a few moments before noticing my *Queen is
Dead* T-shirt. A massive warm smile ripped across his face
which for me was a beautiful, memorable moment. He resembled a lost child in a department store having just spotted his
mother. Walking to the front of the stage, Mike threw me his
drumstick. I never did manage to catch it.

It didn't matter: the queen may have been (long) dead, but
Mike was very much alive and drumming.

GARY MILLAR of Ashton-On-Ribble, Lancashire

As most Smiths tracks are only two minutes seventeen seconds
long, I found I had to act swiftly to dance with the girl who had
caught my eye . . .

Preston's Warehouse Club. Three floors of sweaty, beer-
stained bodies gyrating to everything from Bauhaus and Killing
Joke to The Orb and Björk. I left my drink and had to dance
with that girl again. Bliss – a long one, 'The Queen Is Dead'.
Sponge and a rusty spanner. I had the lot. We strutted and
danced in our strange and pathetic fashion. It felt like an hour
rather than five minutes, then a burst of dry ice, a cough and it
was over. We left the floor as The Cure told us that boys don't
cry. That was just one of many outings to the S.N.S.B.C. – 'Saturday Night Sad Bastards' Club'. Her name was Heather and
her happy, casual manner had hit me like a hammer.

Reel Around The Fountain

MARION FIELDS of Helsinki, Finland

I once spent four months in the middle of nowhere in central Finland doing a course in creative writing. Being midwinter, it was dark for most of each day and snowing constantly. One evening, I started drinking wine with my roommate and soon we decided to go and knock on a friend's door. She was writing a letter to her boyfriend and listening to 'Reel Around The Fountain'. We were joined by her roommate and had a wonderful long conversation about what makes the world go round and what makes life bearable. As the snowflakes fell, we played the tape over and over again ... It was one of those moments when you really felt you belonged somewhere, even though the rest of the small town shunned our college and living there could sometimes be depressing.

GRAHAM COLEMAN of Hampstead, London

I spent the summer of '83 contemplating my first term at university. Mercifully, I had (at last) purged myself of the musical evils of progressive rock and heavy metal which had polluted my A level years. 'Beanos' second-hand record store in Croydon relieved me of a towering, patchouli-scented mound of Deep Purple, AC/DC and Genesis albums. At least they had found a good home, settling in alongside hundreds of identical cousins all selling at low, low prices. If there was one thing I knew about being a student it was that you had to affect a knowledge of obscure indie groups years before they cut a record and preferably weeks before they even formed.

I'd always listened to John Peel's shows and liked The Fall and had a sneaking regard for The Buzzcocks and Joy Division. So when he introduced a new Manchester group in session I taped it and despite the oddest sounding singer I'd heard since, well, Mark E. Smith, I soon came to love the band with a passion.

Oh yes, 'Reel Around The Fountain' was a great tune with pervy lyrics that were a good deal more honest than anything which has ever issued from the pens of hairy-chested heavy metal heroes. 'Fifteen minutes with you . . .' Surely the secret mantra of every world-weary teenage virgin.

IAN GOLDSACK of Maltby, South Yorkshire

I first became aware of The Smiths while wandering around the house at a friend's birthday party. Entering his elder sister's bedroom, I happened upon a file stuffed with photographs and newspaper cuttings concerning the band. At the comprehensive, I'd been aware of older pupils carrying strange records emblazoned with images of unknown people from a bygone age, and had been intrigued.

Plundering the hallowed file, I surveyed with interest the words of this strange creature 'Morrissey' and became quickly and acutely aware of the chords they were striking. At last, something of a kindred spirit!

On Monday I set off for town hellbent on purchasing a record by this band which so fascinated me. *Meat is Murder* turned out to be their latest offering but for some reason I was drawn to the purple-tinted first album bearing their name. I returned home clutching the precious cassette and thus 'Reel

Around The Fountain' became the first Smiths track I was consciously aware of hearing.

At that age, I had probably enjoyed (or endured?) more exposure to pop music than most of my contemporaries. An uncle persistently foisted one 'sixties classic' or another upon me. The Rolling Stones, The Doors, The Byrds, the Velvets and Bob Dylan were names I knew well. Perhaps this is why The Smiths appealed instantly. I was ten years old; New York drug culture meant nothing to me. I hadn't a hope in hell of relating to anything remotely like that. It was all rather faceless, pointless and drab. The Smiths were real. This song was real.

I had found *my* band, and not a moment too soon. 'Reel Around The Fountain' was to coincide with a time of lost innocence. I shall always connect it with the time I was subjected to the contents of a porn magazine which was being passed around the bus. Perhaps we all remember the moment when something pure and innocent was lost forever. I woke up, and didn't much like what I saw. I guess I've been wishing I could go back to sleep ever since.

JULIA RILEY of Newton Centre, Massachusetts

I felt lost and stranded on a strange planet when I came from summer in the north of England to college amidst the auburn-leaved woodlands of somnolent New England. Such was the atmosphere of the place that the students, rather than cultivating their young minds, would go right out of them with depression or aggression. The former was my response. The case of a crazed student who shot and killed several classmates and a teacher may serve as an example of the latter.

This feeling of disorientation and loneliness was not unfamiliar. I had rarely found anyone or anything in life which made me feel any other way. A quiet and diffident youngster, I tended to retreat – trying to shrink myself invisible. I spent days on end studiously avoiding classes and people, half-sleeping and staring apathetically at my hands. I felt sure no one would notice if I died, least of all myself.

Sometimes I'd play the records of David Bowie or Patti Smith, T. Rex or The Who or The Jam. Some of these performers I'd even liked enough to have written about them for fanzines. Their images, which I'd sketched or printed on to T-shirts, were my only conscious statement to the world.

Then one day a fifteen-year-old suedehead engaged me in conversation in the usual way; we got along well and discovered a shared interest in music. Blessedly, boldly she assured me that I had heard nothing yet. I must, she insisted, as a matter of urgency lest I die that dark night, acquaint myself with the beauty of The Smiths. So she took me to her room where (flouting school rules) she'd painted a mural of this special group on to the wall. She sat me down insisting I be silent and listen. Setting the first album on the turntable, she placed the lyric-sheet in my hands.

The tone-arm descended and within five minutes I realised that all the others had been mere opening acts. This person singing, this Morrissey of quiff and beads and emotive, handsome face was to be the main attraction. The things he sang . . . illuminating my darkest fears and most secret desires which had lain in shadow for so long. 'It's time the tale were told of how you took a child and you made him old.'

Drawn though I often was to lyrically expressive artists, I had never heard anyone touch so knowingly – and with exquisite tenderness – upon the hurt and loneliness and passion of other souls. Truly, Morrissey was singing out . . . reaching out. And he connected. I remained silent as the album played on, and when its solemn, graceful closing track ended, I stayed mute – in wonder and awe. 'Maybe,' I dared to think as I lay wide awake in a room in the middle of some old forest, 'maybe I'm on the right planet after all.' Or at the very least on the wrong planet in good company.

Ten years later, Morrissey and his songs retain that power and brilliance. The vital beauty of that life-saving voice will always make me reel.

JIM ALEXANDER of Croftfoot, Glasgow

I sang this! At a party in Dundee. Some guy produced a guitar
and began strumming and a Smiths song seemed the obvious
choice. Initially I was pretty confident I could sing the words to
any Smiths ditty, but that frame of mind came quickly unstuck.
It's amazing how your memory capacity fails – sort of switches
off, power-cut style – when you don't have the actual record
playing to sing along to. Anyway, we eventually stumbled upon
'Reel Around The Fountain' and clarity returned. I sang my
heart out, replacing the word 'haven' with 'heaven' as I'm oft
prone to do. The performance seemed well received. People
clapped. I then proceeded to drink at double speed and, for the
rest of the night, tried to convince anyone unlucky enough to
be within earshot, that Alexander O'Neal's new single was
called 'Shit In A Bucket'. A great night!

ANDREW TAYLOR of Bootle, Liverpool

The Carter family's Bonfire Night party was an annual event
famed throughout the neighbourhood for its ambitious pyro-
technics. This was the '83 edition, however, and of vastly
greater importance to thirsty sixteen year olds was the fact that
there was always gallons of free beer around. We headed out
to the off licence in Kirkby and laid in a token-gesture stash of
24 cans. Then off to the party we went.

But beer wasn't the only thing I was carrying that night.
Knowing that Tom Carter owned a twin-deck, tape-to-tape
stereo, I had begged and borrowed a copy of the now-legendary
Smiths' 'Peel Sessions'. I hassled Tom all night to let me use the
machine, so determined was I to get my own copy of those
wonderful songs. True to form, he came across and we ventured
up to his bedroom to do the taping.

Tom's younger sister Michelle interrupted as we listened
to 'Reel Around The Fountain', enquiring as to why we'd swapped the downstairs sounds of Lionel Richie for 'that load of

miserable nonsense'. She had no idea! The Smiths meant little
or nothing to Tom either, but thanks to him I had my precious
copy of the 'Peel Sessions' a full year before the release of *Hatful of Hollow*. Cheers Tom!

JIM O'DONOGHUE of Cricklewood, London

My sister's eighteenth birthday party. I am nearly three years
her senior, but have never had sex with anyone or anything, unless you count the abortive mutual-masturbation sessions with
long-fingered schoolfriend Jim. Unless you count the nights of
furry, platonic intimacy with my big white pet rabbit. The formal part of the evening is over, and my sister's friends lounge
vogueishly around our candlelit sitting-room listening to The
Smiths' debut album. This is Nottingham in the late eighties;
the girls (and the guest list is composed mainly of girls, save for
a few university mates of mine) wear alluring black leggings
and crossover Next tops. I harbour urgent aspirations towards
most of them.

Hearing this song now, it recalls with painful clarity the
half-baked nature of my ambitions concerning the tiny, pink-cheeked creatures I once believed women to be. Always half-right
and half-wrong ... and missing by light years the promised
absolute those encounters were supposed to yield. The climax
that never, somehow, came.

A mile to the south, trains are rattling tantalisingly across the
tracks. Under dank canal bridges, white stilettos clash sexily
with white trainers. My own lust is a dysfunctional thing –
bereft of point or purpose. But when my best friend steps outside with Claudie, that mistimed, misfiring desire is given a
goal: I want this girl!

Doubtless, juvenile sex is three parts ego-tripping. Neglecting
her friend, upon whom any advances would be met with eager
reciprocation, I crawl under the piano where cowers Claudie,
free once more from the clumsy hands of silly university boys.

One despairing, the other desperate, we enjoy a kiss whose contact is scarcely real.

Every one of the words rang true – I lapped it up. Inadequacy's justification, as Morrissey points out, is the sad but pretty harmony one makes of it afterwards. But punish yourself to bring its truth to life; the nasty powerplay of public snogging. 'People see no worth in you, oh but I do.'

Yep, the memory of that night appalls me. Friendships were fucked up. But the grandiloquence of the line 'It's time the tale were told' confers upon my stupidity some measure of twisted beauty. I can listen to it now and still the pretty, wordy self-delusions return to tempt. These mistakes we made were ugly and pathetic but, hell, they made for dandy stories!

MARCO BILYK of Basingstoke, Hampshire

Up until around early 1985, I hated The Smiths, or rather I pretended to. I don't know why, I just did. I'd seen Morrissey on *Top of the Pops* messing around with flowers and somehow I got it into my head that I should steer clear of this band. I think it was jealousy or something. Anyway, on a balmy summer afternoon in 1984, I remember sitting in my friend John's bedroom while he played me *Hatful of Hollow*. Although keen not to show it, I was secretly impressed with what I was hearing – well most of it. I did find 'How Soon Is Now?', 'Back To The Old House' and 'Please Please Please Let Me Get What I Want' slightly tedious on initial plays. 'Reel Around The Fountain', however, frustrated me and yet captured my interest. One day I could listen to it in its entirety, on another I would fast-forward it to near the end. I was intrigued with the story it told; reeling around a fountain and being slapped on a patio. I was seventeen at the time and it just seemed such a mysterious and evocative song whose lyrics beguiled me. Although not an instantly accessible tune, it has an enduring quality which, whenever I hear it now, means it's like hearing it for the first time. 'Reel Around The Fountain' recalls an interesting and awkward period of my life, a personal watershed perhaps, and the coming to terms with it.

Rubber Ring

BEN E. LILLY of Alpharetta, Georgia, USA

Presbyterian College in Clinton, South Carolina is wedged between a 'Margaret's-More-To-Love' outsize clothing store for women and a beat-up country gas station. Not the typical setting for an introduction to The Smiths, but it's where I found myself in the winter of 1988. Living in a single dorm room on the top floor of the then dilapidated 'Spencer Hall'. I grew terribly homesick and lonely. From my window, the view was of a grimy water tower standing among an endless span of leafless trees. It did little to cheer me up.

One of the few friendships I formed during the first semester was with a stylish outcast named Angela Forest. Angela was thin, stood around five feet seven inches tall and spoke in an unobtrusive Midwestern accent. She favoured wide-brimmed hats and flowery dresses and thus looked visibly out of place on a campus where the uniform for girls seemed to be T-shirt and jeans.

Angela and I had met in a maths class and discovered a common bond in our feelings of being trapped in a small town. Neither of us were interested in the fraternity, or the drinking and drug scene come to that. To our despair, the isolated surroundings offered little else in the way of social activities.

Late at night, Angela and I would often find ourselves standing in the middle of the campus howling at the winter sky about our homesickness. She would bring her little Sony cassette player and we would listen to The Smiths for hours as we talked. 'Rubber Ring' was a track which always seemed especially pertinent to our situation. For some reason, the jubilant music in the context of our mutual commiseration would start us laughing – almost every time. Those strange nights helped us through that long semester.

As the weeks ran into months, we both formalised plans to transfer to other colleges. After leaving Presbyterian College, we lost touch and I've heard nothing of Angela for several years. But the words and music of The Smiths have been a constant throughout.

Seven years on, as I'm dancing and laughing and finally living, I often wonder what became of her. I'd love to think that somewhere next to a wide-brimmed hat and a flowery dress there's a Smiths tape playing away in a little portable cassette recorder.

GAYE HUTCHINSON of Maltby, South Yorkshire

An underestimated classic! On Friday nights in the pubs of Maltby I sing this repeatedly . . . in my head. I adore the line 'When you lay in awe on the bedroom floor . . .' In context it isn't especially sexual, but Morrissey's delivery is so erotic. I often imagine myself lying on my rather worn bedroom carpet panting with sexual exhaustion after having had Morrissey over for tea.

And admittedly, it has been known for me to appear outside loved ones' windows at the dead of night, desperately wailing, 'Do you love me like you used to?'

JENNY PARKIN of Huddersfield, West Yorkshire

I bought *The World Won't Listen* on an overcast afternoon in Huddersfield, when I was fourteen. I skipped school and trundled alone into town, on the 236 from Barnsley, after spending the morning poncing around in the art room, trying to look gothicky, and later on, poncing around on a hockey pitch, trying to stay away from the ball. I went for Harmony hair dye and maybe some more black stuff to wear. So how I ended up with my first Smiths record, I'm not sure. It was a 'Nice Price' red sticker sort of bargain affair, and I was curious about this band, whose T-shirts adorned all the floppy-haired sixth form boys. My younger brother, now in the sixth form at the same school, has claimed my grey *Queen is Dead* T-shirt as his own. Some things stay the same. 'Rubber Ring' is still my favourite – I did a lot of lying in awe on the bedroom floor at that age. And I would put my elbows on the table at dinnertime in the school canteen, talking knowledgeably about The Smiths, like I knew loads about music, and how Morrissey probably even knew me to say hello to.

JAMES ROYLE of Peterborough, Cambridgeshire

I am sure (following the lines of probability) such an experience has occurred but I am cursed with a memory that cannot hold dates and times. How I envy those people who vividly recall their first Smiths song, where they were, who was there, what they had for tea beforehand and what number the track reached in the charts!

I do, however, know that since I was approximately sixteen, I have suffered the normal adolescent angst, left home, lost many jobs, met the girl who later became my wife (who danced with me to 'Panic' at our wedding reception), been in hospital many times, lost some very good friends and gained some more, experienced some marvellous highs and depressing lows, and generally experienced the normal everyday drudge.

But, throughout all of the above that constitutes that last seven odd years of my existence, the most constant entity in my life has been the music, the words and the life of Morrissey. So, as I say, some such occurrence must have taken place.

Actually, just thrashing that above monologue out has proved to me that I don't actually need to have some fantastic/sad/
meaningful story because I know that whatever high and low
times I may have had, The Smiths and Morrissey have always
been around – which is good enough for me.

A Rush And A Push And The Land Is Ours

TOM GALLAGHER of Giffnock, Glasgow

In the summer of '87, Martin and I set off for London to spend a week with Big Davie who had, earlier that year, found a job in the capital. Lurking at the back of my head was the vague notion to do likewise but I did not seriously expect to be away from Glasgow any longer than seven days – a view shared by those in whom I confided. The opportunity to prove them wrong was both unexpected and pretty terrifying. I recall going to a bar agency in Regent Street fully anticipating being shown the door on grounds of youth and/or inexperience. Quite unknown to me, live-in pub jobs came ten-a-penny at that time, and any number of vacancies were up for grabs. My posting was to be the very big and very busy Prince Alfred in Bayswater where I was plunged headlong into the mad, bad, hazy twilight world that is live-in London barwork.

The months which followed had a disjointed surrealism about them as I worked long hours through the summer heat and got drunk and met Simone and developed a taste for greyhound racing and stayed up all night so very many times. I remember them also for the constant, numbing exposure to the music beloved of London's white ethnic travelling population – The Pogues, U2, Men At Work et al. Not being possessed of a decent cassette player, The Smiths were almost forgotten . . .

Autumn came and we ended up in Cambridge. I served up

the tomato juices and vermouths at the small but pretentious Gonville Hotel. Simone, for her part, dished out pots of tea and buttered scones at the Corn Exchange. We met infrequently back at the small flat. As relationships go, this one had the kind of star quality which so often accompanies that which is precious, fragile and utterly doomed. Circumstances conspired to render it no more authentic than toddlers playing mummies and daddies in a Wendy house. Besides, all too soon she would return to New South Wales and to university and I would trudge back to real life. Both of us knew this, despite the plans and the promises.

This, of course, was the time of *Strangeways . . .* release. 'The Smiths! God, yes, I remember them . . .' A previous life? And I bought it and played it and on hearing 'A Rush And A Push . . .' knew instantly that things had changed irrevocably. The band, the sound, the lyrics had grown up, matured, become cynical and knowing. The poignance was overwhelming, for in the 'mystical time-zone' of those few months I knew I'd been doing exactly the same.

BRIAN MATTHEWS of Camberley, Surrey

The night after purchasing The Smiths' farewell album, I had a vivid dream. The ghostly figure of a suffragette visited the ghostly figure of Margaret Thatcher in her study. Rolling her eyes skyward, the suffragette told Thatcher, 'You've made such an evil mess, I could almost believe you're a man.'

I can only attribute this bizarre scene to earlier, repeated playings of 'A Rush And A Push . . .'

Rusholme Ruffians

TOM GALLAGHER of Giffnock, Glasgow

We never did have any balls. Anyone who has ever played ping-pong in a sixth form common-room will know that the table might as well be turned over to shove-halfpenny. Trying to find a ball most mornings is not unlike prospecting for gold in Peckham. Bored and listless, we shunned shove-halfpenny, preferring instead to sit around and smoke and affect sophistication.

Dave Blockley managed this better than most; he positively starred at it. I guess it was just practice. Dave had been dating girls when the rest of us were yet content to spend evenings stealing frogs and pulling the legs off hubcaps.

Dave owned a guitar and sported turn-ups on his trousers. In 1984-5 turn-ups were unheard of outside the ranks of Condor-scented octogenarians. He talked of becoming a tailor and taught me how to cuff the bottom of one's trousers – advice for which I was enormously grateful.

Numbered prominently among Dave's other passions were his battered Hillman Avenger and Lloyd Cole And The Commotions. When not otherwise engaged, he'd moan/warble his doleful way through the band's paper-thin repertoire.

Surprisingly, his knowledge of The Smiths was scarcely more than cosmetic. Those very few songs to which he could provide the lyrics were invariably delivered à la Cole, which in truth was as near as I got attempting to impersonate Morrissey. He could never resist paraphrasing; none but the strongest of lyrics was safe from his inventive whimsy. 'Rusholme Ruffians' was one song to undergo the Blockley treatment. 'Scratch my name on your arm with an old tin can,' he'd croon to my annoyance. But it stuck, as these things are wont to do. And still does.

Who the hell said anything about a fountain pen anyway? Fountain pen . . .? Fetch me the lyric-sheet!

SARAH BRADBURY of New Moston, Manchester

Everyone in Manchester goes to the fairs when they come to town. This song might've been written about an experience I had at one such fair in my neighbourhood in '93. A group of us went along and one lad got mugged and ended up in a really bad way with numerous bruises and a black eye. A friend of mine would have been jumped and bottled by a gang of girls had her boyfriend not intervened. The whole atmosphere that night simmered and bubbled with violence.

The line about the skirt ascending is so true of Manchester fairs. A short skirt will get you plenty of free rides, and this opportunity is seized upon by many of the females there.

JENNIFER BRUNDAGE of San Jose, California, USA

For a while I considered simply writing Morrissey's name on my arm, but didn't have a fountain pen with which to do it. A magic marker seemed a distressing alternative, so I never did get around to it.

PATRICK LEE of Harrow, Middlesex

I am now in my thirties and have been an avid Smiths fan for many intriguing years.

It is my contention that the power and daring contained within the work of Morrissey and Marr is unrivalled to this day. I like to think of The Smiths as an upbeat black comedy ensemble as opposed to the blanket misery guts tag used so often to describe the attitude of the band.

Anyway, on with the story. I hail from a small town called Dundalk in the Republic of Ireland and on 11 February 1986, The Smiths came to town. The venue was the pretty awful Fairway Hotel, usually home to dire disco music and the dance around your handbag brigade. However, on this occasion the place was transformed into a flower-bedecked celebration. The Smiths played a howling set, the highlight of which was the rasping rendition of 'Rusholme Ruffians'/'Marie's The Name (His Latest Flame)'. This song has remained a personal favourite ever since and when on my turntable (à la *Rank*) still evokes stirring memories of being young, rebellious and cool on that incredible winter's night in Ireland.

To this day my Smiths addiction has not waned and I certainly feel lucky to have grown up enjoying the work of such an historic band. Thanks for the memories Moz & co.

MURDO GILLIES of Shawbost, Isle-of-Lewis

I was living in a flat with three other guys who were all fellow students. Friday nights were the highlight of the week – breaking up the dreary round of college work and impoverishment. The flat itself was known to all and sundry as 'The Fridge', for it was generally warmer outside which, in Aberdeen, is saying plenty. So Fridays found us, without fail, drinking and thawing out in one of two student pubs in town.

One time, the invitation to a party was extended and we duly had a whip round with which to buy a few beers for later. On arrival, the place wasn't too busy although everyone seemed to be having a good time. After an hour or so, someone suggested I change the music and scanning what was available, I was delighted to spot a copy of *Meat is Murder*. Seconds after placing it on the turntable, I was confronted by a bloke demanding to know what the hell I was doing, putting on 'this load of shit'. It became instantly obvious that he didn't give a damn about the music but was simply intent on a fight. Appeals to reason were never going to have the desired effect so I told him to piss off.

After having been hit on the face for sticking on this pacifist music, I looked up to see him start on someone else before pulling a knife in the realisation that he'd soon be outnumbered. At this, it seemed a good idea to let him make good his exit. Outside, he proceeded to cut a passer-by on the back of the head with a spade and plunge a rake through a car windscreen.

The whole unpleasant incident comes to mind every time I decide to give *Meat is Murder* an airing and hear the opening bars of 'Rusholme Ruffians'.

Sheila Take A Bow

MARIAN COLE of Brooklyn, New York, USA

I had a huge poster of the single's sleeve long before I was able to find the record itself. (I was in school in a very small town and UK imports were very difficult to come by.) Anyway, I was living with an opera singer at the time – big blonde hair, all red lips – very exaggeratedly feminine. She looked exactly like 'Candy Darling', the character on the sleeve and on my poster. She hated that poster . . . if the stunning likeness wasn't enough, her name was Sheila!

SANDRA McMAHON of Wythenshawe, Manchester

I had started back at work after a maternity break and my daughter was being looked after by my mother. Our house at that time was very much a 'Smiths' house – myself and three younger brothers were all massive fans and at any time you could bet there'd be an album or a video playing. Arriving home one day, Jade (aged six months) was perched in her rocking-cradle, bouncing away and happily muttering 'She bow, She bow!' and to this day we all joke that these were her very first words. Ten years on, and Take That are firm favourites . . .

All Men Have Secrets

RUSS C. S. THOMAS of Ferndale, South Wales

Working in Cardiff's HMV store, we received a consignment on the day of release which featured 'You Just Haven't Earned It Yet, Baby' erroneously on the A-side. We happily sold oodles of them until about lunchtime when a harassed phone call from Rough Trade demanded their re-call. They're probably pretty collectable now . . . Are they? I've got one!

EDD TRAVERS of Kirkintilloch, Nr Glasgow

Some friends and I attended a Smiths night in Glasgow when we were around seventeen. At that time there was a big guy in our year at school called Johnny who was extremely quiet and shy and generally went about on his own. Anyway, we knew he liked The Smiths so decided to ask him along. We got to the pub which was pretty busy, drank a bit, danced a bit and generally had a few laughs. Throughout all this, Johnny said little, which of course surprised us none. Cometh the hour, however . . .

'Sheila Take A Bow' came on and Johnny went haywire! He stormed on to the dancefloor, ripping his shirt off and swirling it manically around his head. This was a different person – not the quiet, reserved guy we'd started out with. Johnny was really *living* it, if you know what I mean. He was really out there, on that Smiths vibe. We all screamed and cheered and danced along for the rest of the night. Everyone around was smiling – everyone understood. I remember thinking how happy I was, and wanting that night to go on forever. It was such a buzz to be, for once, among people who knew where I was coming from. I still think of Johnny when I hear this song.

JOANNE O'GRADY of Booterstown, County Dublin

Don't laugh, but this plays and I think of billowing shirts on a washing line in the manner of a very naff washing powder

advertisement ... The summer breeze, a fresh meadow ... I
said don't laugh!

Shoplifters Of The World Unite

Ms NICK BURTON of Braunstone Town, Leicester

For a long time I was convinced that this song's lyric included the line, 'Try living in the real world, instead of Cheltenham.' It therefore took on a whole new coloration, due entirely to a mishearing.

Incidentally, Cheltenham never did seem like the real world to me – especially the new shopping complex! 'Shoplifters . . .' sends up the yuppie myth which hallmarked the eighties, and finds Moz at his most delightfully Cowardesque and playful. The song just cries out for accompanying cigarette holder gesticulations.

JOHN DOWER of Glasgow, Scotland

I missed The Smiths. I didn't discover them until late 1990. In fact I must have been one of the very few students who arrived at university not knowing who they were.

My eighties were spent in London suburbia smoking dope and listening to Jimi Hendrix, Pink Floyd and The Rolling Stones. These musical tastes were further refined . . . Supertramp, Fleetwood Mac, The Doobie Brothers (though in rare moments of sophistication we would dabble with The Beatles' *White Album*). I didn't raid my dad's wardrobe for large white shirts as I already had an established street style: Bjorn Bjorg Diadoras, deerstalker, bleached denim jeans, Pringle lambswool jumper, Lacoste cotton T-shirt and Tacchini tracksuit top (the distance is clear . . . try imagining Morrissey in the crimson and navy blue shiny gloss of Sergio Tacchini).

Indiedom was a distant world not to be entered until the arrival of The Stone Roses and by then it had entangled itself with dance music.

Unwittingly I came into contact with it at the end of the eighties. In 1989 I shared a table on an Intercity with what I later realised to be an indie girl. Earnestly I was told how she liked 1950s black and white films and James Dean; why sometimes people need to go mad, take off their clothes and jump in the canal; how stealing from Safeways was justifiable. Nodding across the table I thought, 'Stupid bitch, you think stealing Mars bars is cool?'

Three years later in Glasgow, I heard my first Smiths song – 'Shoplifters Of The World Unite' – and visions of British Rail formica just outside Preston rushed back.

GILL of Rochdale, Lancashire

I can't really remember a time when I didn't listen to The Smiths. Throughout my various phases in music they were always in the background, the first thing I would listen to when fed up. Everyone would say, 'No wonder you're fed up listening to that,' but everything about The Smiths made me feel better. My only regret was never going to see them.

It would be impossible to explain in words how I feel about the music except to say nothing has or ever will be as good; in my opinion the songs are timeless.

'Shoplifters . . .' reminds me of early February this year. I was so excited to hear that Morrissey was touring, but slightly disappointed to discover he wasn't playing in Manchester. The nearest venue for me was Blackpool so I desperately tried to find another Mozza fan to go with me. My best friend Jeanette came up with the idea of staying over in Blackpool and having a couple of days there before the gig. Great idea, I thought. There was no way I could get time off work – so I thought I'd conveniently be ill for a couple of days. We got the tickets and booked a B&B and were really looking forward to it.

The weeks seemed to drag but eventually Wednesday 8 February came. I had decided to drive, hoping my unreliable old car would behave. It started snowing that morning so we set off early, armed with flask, food and enough clothes for a fortnight.

To cut a long story short the car broke down on a roundabout near work! We eventually got there by train with a few more minor mishaps on the way. The gig was brilliant, well worth the hassle – Morrissey sang 'Shoplifters . . .' and I compared myself to them – risking everything for my 'fix', but I'd do it again tomorrow. Including the car bill and bad hangover!

Some Girls Are Bigger Than Others

LOUISE BARNES of Stretford, Manchester

This song evokes memories of a summer holiday spent with two
close friends in a Newquay guesthouse. During our stay we met
an abundance of friends but made two enemies. This came
about due to our letting a boy sleep in the room for a night – he
was stranded after losing his friends in a club. A certain couple
(whose hostility we sensed every morning over the toast and
cornflakes) happened to spot our guest and decided to snitch on
us. Consequently, the landlady nearly threw us out. Later that
day, I played *The Queen is Dead* several times with particular
emphasis on 'Some Girls . . .', my special favourite. Entirely by
coincidence, the snitchers across the landing were rather large
people and the woman thought we were out to antagonise her.
I nearly ended up flying through the window and into the foam-
ing briny beyond. Only by convincing her of my passion for the
song was this narrowly avoided! 'Some Girls . . .' still makes me
smile as I remember her scarlet puffy face, the flailing fat arms
and that enormous looming bust.

PAUL MARTIN of Leicester

I hate this song. I expected a choir of angels and a fanfare
of brass . . . Instead I got 'Some Girls . . .' and hypothermia.

167

Typical. Nowadays, I'll only listen to it when held at gunpoint, because on hearing this wretched song (it's popular in supermarkets, you know) I am instantly catapulted back to a certain bittersweet time in my life.

Around the tail end of the eighties, short of money and employment prospects, I awoke one afternoon to find myself stumbling haphazardly into the throes of what can only be described as a relationship . . .

For a short while we made Antony and Cleopatra look like Mavis and Derek, although it's doubtful whether we'd have caused Barbara 'Bonecrusher' Cartland many sleepless nights. Let's face it – love on the dole is an uphill struggle. While lovers everywhere clamour for pearls and fine wine, one can but feign anti-materialism and offer a chip butty by way of comparison.

And the dole age dragged on. And on. Eventually we grew tired of watching the rising damp assume fascinating kaleidoscopic patterns on the wall and went our separate ways. I suppose ennui can get a little boring after a time. And no – I haven't seen her since.

Such topsy-turvy times deserve more steadfast a soundtrack than 'Some Girls . . .' and quite why this song should remain so near the knuckle escapes me to this day. Claptrap for an emotional complex? Very probably – perhaps this explains why the curtains are still drawn. Whatever the reason, I know this vacuous, relentless and entirely pointless song will continue to tantalise and terrorise me in much the same way that a bluebottle evades the lunging swipes of a rolled up *Daily Mirror*. Still, we live and learn, and I suppose some of my happiest times have been spent squeezing the seventeenth cup from an old tea bag. I love this song!

EDDIE PARSLEY of Kidlington, Oxfordshire

It's true. My sister Ruth was always bigger than her friend. But then, her mum was always bigger than our mum. I still laugh when I listen to this song; it makes me happy which is rare these days.

CALUM McGILP of Studland, Dorset

Utterly surreal . . . I can imagine Richard Burton singing this to Elizabeth Taylor while opening a crate of Welsh ale. Christ! Who am I to talk?

CHRISTOPHE NEFF of Limeil Brevannes, France

I knew The Smiths with *The Queen is Dead* which was not so bad for a young French boy who could not rely on the media to provide such out-of-law music. At that time, my girlfriend had left me after I'd enjoyed many months of love with this fat but nice girl. I was so disappointed that I would listen to this song all the time. In French, 'fat' and 'big' are translated as the same word, so it helped me to persuade myself that she was not so great anyway. And since then, I've never been out with fatties.

SOPHIE LEGENCHE of Neuville-Sur-Oise, France

Ten o'clock on a Saturday night in the centre of Paris; not easy to find a quiet place to have a drink and a chat. We end up in a pavement café. A group of boys sitting near us suddenly become quite animated. Miracle! One of them has just discovered the difference between what you call the 'waist' and the 'hips', which he illustrates with many gestures. His friends are simply amazed by his earth-shattering discovery and so are we!

HANNAH of Bath, Avon

My dad told me of a person he'd been introduced to at a party who loved The Smiths and who was a deadringer for Morrissey.

My first thought was that he clearly couldn't be all *that* devout or he would have been home like me and not at a party! I dismissed him from my mind on the assumption that I wouldn't like him much.

A few dreary weeks passed until, wonder of wonders, I myself received an invite to a similar get-together. Well, not so similar, actually . . . this one boasted a seventies theme. My friend and I arrived, looking and feeling like fools, but blending with the sartorial idiocy surprisingly well, none the less. We drank and drank – taking refuge in the age-old cure for awkwardness.

At the height of my stupor I was introduced to the person of whom Dad had spoken, and was surprised to find we got on well, spending the remainder of the party together and exchanging numbers at the end. Over the following months we became good friends – wearing one another's T-shirts and discussing Smiths lyrics. But all too soon he moved away to university and although Her Majesty's postal service did us proud, I missed him a lot.

That November, my birthday rolled around and among the usual parcels, there arrived a very big box bearing his city's postcode. Inside there was a huge white pillow with the words, 'Send me your pillow, the one that you dream on,' scrawled across. It summed up my feelings exactly, and I couldn't wait to go to bed that night!

ALAN McBEATH of Stonehaven, Grampian

Years back, sometime around 1986, I found myself on a college training scheme and living in digs in Dundee. My worldly possessions amounted to virtually nothing, which was probably a blessing spacewise since my roommate's utterly massive record collection spread itself into every available nook and cranny. On the day we moved in, everything I owned was accommodated in a small sports holdall. My mate, meantime, was pulling up outside in a works van whose axles were creaking under the weight of music system and box after box of LPs and twelve-inch singles.

His habit of an evening was to disappear off to the local boozer and, being short of cash and a bit of a loner, I was generally invited to rummage through the boxes in his absence. The passport I enjoyed to this wonderful world of music compensated more than somewhat for those many nights spent in, alone.

Being a confirmed republican, I suppose it was entirely natural that one of the very first sleeves to arouse my interest should have been *The Queen is Dead* by The Smiths. The initial playing was interrupted almost immediately by someone at the door, so the first track I really got to listen to was this one. 'I'll have some more of this,' said I to myself and promptly replaced the needle for a second run through. Laughing out loud, it was a curious introduction to a band who I'd later learn were known as 'miserable bastards'.

In the weeks and months which followed, I increasingly accompanied my music guru to the district's alehouses for drunken singalongs in which 'Some Girls ...' invariably figured.

Still III

LOUISE BARNES of Stretford, Manchester

Sometime in 1990, at the tender age of fourteen, I found myself
on a fluffy white settee with a spotty contemporary – his parents
were out. What an achievement! He was rewinding a tape. I recall the uncomfortable feeling of wishing he'd remove the
hideous turquoise tracksuit top and keep his hands to himself!
Anyway, he played this tape and remarked on the 'depressing'
nature of the content. So what? I found it uplifting and the lyric
seemed to be about *me*. The iron bridge which I crossed every
cloudy day. I was fascinated and entranced and scarcely noticed
his cloying kisses. I was in love – not with the boy but with this
phenomenal band. This love, I knew, would never abandon me.
The only tears I would shed would be on account of its beautiful truth. I felt secure. My turquoise-clad romeo would wave
goodbye but *my* hand was snug within The Smiths glove.

MATTEO B. BIANCHI of Milan, Italy

I guess my story concerns The Smiths' very first album but for
me, of those ten songs, this one is perhaps the most significant.

Ever since childhood, my main interests have always been music and literature; I was never the kind of boy who spent his time
fighting and playing soccer with the other children. I preferred to

remain in my room, reading. Needless to say, most of the teachers adored me for this while the other boys branded me a 'sissy'. Growing up, things were to change a little. By the age of fifteen, being a good student was no longer something to be ashamed of. Having said that, my taste in music still made me different. I was the only one of my class who was interested in bands such as Depeche Mode, Haircut 100 and Japan. For this reason, rather than the academic side of things, I was still openly considered eccentric. Those around me stuck firmly with Italian pop and occasionally ventured into areas obviously suggested by their elder brothers: Bob Dylan, Pink Floyd, The Police, etc. Being the oldest of my family, I had nobody's lead to follow – nobody's records to borrow. I had to find them myself. At the time new wave were the key words for me. My school diary was filled with photographs cut from the music magazines. Those in colour tended to be the best – Adam And The Ants, Culture Club, even A Flock Of Seagulls! I clearly remember a guy flicking through that diary and asking me, 'Duran Duran – what kind of a fucking name for a band is that?' I suppose it wasn't an inappropriate question.

One morning a pal named Marco Molinari came up to me with a record in his hands. 'A friend gave me this album,' he said, 'do you know them?' I looked at the cover and was surprised to see the image of a naked man. The name of the band was not new to me, but I'd never heard any of their songs. 'No, actually I don't know them,' I said. 'Can I take a look?' It was the first time I'd held a Smiths record. I looked closely at the cover, read the song titles and finally began to scan the lyrics. It was a shock. 'England is mine and it owes me a living/But ask me why and I'll spit in your eye . . .' I couldn't believe how accurately that mirrored my feelings. OK, so this was Italy, not England, but the same thought had crossed my mind on many occasions. Soon I reached the line, 'Does the body rule the mind . . .' and this rang equally true at a time when my first real sexual impulses were beginning to surface. After all, this was my everyday doubt! The Smiths were, and always will be, the only band I grew to love *before* hearing the music.

Morrissey's lyrics were to have a profound effect on me. Gradually, I forgot about the new wave stuff at a time when pictures of Duran Duran were beginning to appear in the diaries of schoolfriends. Of course, changes are never a one-way trip.

Through the songs of The Smiths, I realised I was growing older and needed records and books which reflected more of myself and my needs. It was at this time that I discovered Pier Vittorio Tondelli. He was a new, young Italian writer. I hadn't read any of his books but knew of him through the columns of a musical magazine called *Rockstar*. His was a literary column entitled Culture Club. This I enjoyed very much and was thrilled one day to find his entire piece dedicated not to books but to Morrissey and The Smiths. It was a very clever article, written with humour, and it wasn't difficult to discern Tondelli's admiration for the band. It was the sign I'd been waiting for.

I began to read the novels of Pier Vittorio Tondelli and soon realised that this was the literature I'd been seeking. His books contained stories of love, freedom, sex, desperation, hope, youth and of course, music. So here I was, with my favourite band and my new, favourite writer and unbelievably, there was a deep link between them.

I was very lucky, because I had the chance to meet Pier and become his friend. We would go out together to drink and talk of books, movies and music – mostly The Smiths. He often referred to Morrissey as a genius (a 'bloody genius' were his precise words, if my translation is correct). Pier was fascinated by Morrissey's ability to express so much on the relatively limited canvas of a popular song. Pier died a year after our first meeting, of that horrible, four-letter disease which is killing so many of our best minds throughout the world. His last novel, *Separated Rooms*, is now translated almost everywhere. It tells of a desperate love story between two men, one of whom knows he is about to die. Only after Pier's death did we realise that it was, in fact, autobiographical. The last page of the book starts with a quote from Morrissey: 'I'm so glad to grow older, to move away from those younger years.' Now, when I read it, it seems so natural that he chose the words of that bloody genius to close his last novel.

Today, Tondelli is a cult figure for young people in Italy. Some time ago, I answered an advertisement looking for admirers of his. It transpired that a vast network existed of people keeping his memory alive – writing and meeting and sending messages. And do you know what? Most of them love The Smiths, too. I guess there are some things you just can't explain, some things you must feel to understand.

Next time they ask you why you love The Smiths, just spit in their eyes.

PATRICK CLAEYS of Blankenberge, Belgium

I've always been fascinated with England – it gives us so much good music and so many brilliant groups. When the debut album came out, I dreamt of living in England, even though it wouldn't necessarily owe ME a living!

CLARE GOUDY of Brighton, Sussex

This song will forever be linked in my mind with a disastrous day trip to France that I made with a Canadian friend who was over visiting England. We had been writing to one another for almost a year, and on his arrival I felt that nothing could possibly mar the time we planned to spend together. Sadly, I was soon to be disabused of this notion by the growing animosity which developed between us within a short week.

Perhaps I viewed the French excursion as a possible watershed in relations, and resolved to be as easy-going and civil as possible while on foreign soil. Our sortie across the Channel, however, was doomed from the outset. He had brought along no money, and between us we had little clue as to how to amuse ourselves in a strange city equipped with only a smattering of

French and less than 100 francs. Our return ferry was booked for tea time, but by noon we'd run out of civil conversation and were on to the arguments – rather like something from *Coronation Street*. Time dragged by painfully as we trudged the same street 50 times until by two o'clock we wanted only to rejoin the ferry queue of wine-laden English trippers. Escape!

Once up the gangplank he disappeared, leaving me with only my walkman for company. 'Still Ill' seemed to be the most beautiful song on earth and as the sky darkened I watched France fade from view. Despite the fact that I'd just lost a very good friend, I felt almost happy to feel the wind whip my hair as the waves tossed the boat to and fro.

Stop Me If You Think You've Heard This One Before

CHARLOTTE HALL of Leith, Edinburgh

Before going off to university, and while I was still a bedroom-dwelling Smiths fan with no real friends, I began corresponding with someone in Glasgow. We became good friends on paper, and eventually arranged to meet by the Smiths records in Virgin, Union Street, during my first (miserable) week at university.

His name was B (too shy to be revealed, I think), and he told me that he was gay. Looming large in the background, however, was his powerful girlfriend who would certainly have gubbed him senseless had he revealed his true nature to her. This song reminds me of him: 'Who said I lied, because I never . . .' Although exactly what a shy bald Buddhist's got to do with anything I've never been quite sure.

BOZ BOORER of Camden Town, London

En route to New York to play Madison Square Garden, Spencer's brother, who was sitting next to me on the plane, could take no more. Desperate to satiate his nicotine craving, he took off for the rear of the cabin in order to find some kind soul who might let him sit down to grab a fag.

He was almost out of options as he neared the toilets. Row after row of smug smokers crammed together, puffing away, happy as Larry. He was resigned to the fact that this was going to be a quite miserable flight.

Suddenly, by what seemed like a small miracle, a girl got up and made for the loo. Spying his chance, Spencer's brother hastily approached the vacant space. The bloke in the next seat along looked up and caught his eye.

'Mind if I grab a quick smoke, mate? I'm gasping!' averred Spencer's brother.

'Not at all,' said the bloke, obviously aware of Spencer's brother's plight.

Between one thing and another they got talking. Spencer's brother was only too happy to chat as, if for no other reason, he intended to prolong this smoke-fest for as long as was humanly possible.

'Where are you off to?' asked the bloke.

'Madison Square Garden, actually.'

'Really? What for?'

'Well, my brother plays drums in a band.'

'Who for?' quizzed the bloke, becoming genuinely interested.

'Morrissey.'

'Oh,' said the bloke. 'I used to play drums for Morrissey.'

Little did Spencer's brother know, but he had in fact been chewing the fat with none other than Mike Joyce, who was gigging at the time with the Buzzcocks.

Stretch Out And Wait

MARY DAVIS of Margate, Kent

The loss of my virginity was a far from memorable occasion. I'd spent the first half of my teens wondering, as do most adolescents, what it was all about and would it change my life? My thoughts (delusions?) were centred around idealistic, Cartland-esque images of love, romance and eternity. This song portrays sex for what it can be, but never is in the books and films – messy, uncomfortable and a device for disillusionment. Morrissey reminds us that nudity between lovers is less about bulging biceps and tanned bodies than the fear of our imperfections being found laughable. I adore the honest brutality of this song – summing up the early fumblings we're destined to cringe at as the years pass and a kind of pseudo-sophistication sets in.

I recall hearing 'Stretch Out And Wait' shortly after my first time and being painfully aware that Morrissey was saying, 'I told you so . . .'

MARION FIELDS of Helsinki, Finland

When I was seventeen, the most unlikely radio station in Helsinki decided to broadcast a Smiths concert. Naturally, I waited beside the radio, the tape ready in the recorder. I did, however, have some inkling that the station knew little of what was to come, for that day's programme guide billed the concert as 'American-style rock 'n' roll at its best'.

Perhaps my suspicions were proved right: a General Election was in the offing, and it transpired that the National Coalition Party had bought up all available advertising time during the broadcast. I know that The Smiths weren't *overtly* political, but this can hardly have been their most cost-effective exercise – the NCP are Finland's equivalent of the British Conservative Party. I thought of all the Morrissey interviews I'd read and giggled just a little . . .

I knew all of the songs which were played that night, except for the last one, which impressed me with its air of intimacy – 'Stretch Out And Wait'. I played it a lot afterwards, even if the tape quality was pretty dreadful.

Suffer Little Children

Ms NICK BURTON of Braunstone Town, Leicester

About to embark on my first serious reading of Orwell's *Nineteen Eighty-Four*, I decided a soundtrack would enhance things and 'Heaven Knows I'm Miserable Now' seemed absolutely perfect. It even bore the correct release date! I rummaged through a pile of singles at a local second-hand shop and found it. By mistake, I played the flip-side first, only to discover it even more applicable than my intended choice.

The ghost-like fragility of the song symbolises an old way of life being lost forever. Very Orwellian. Plaintive cries of 'Find me – nothing more . . .' contrast starkly with the notion of an all-seeing, all-powerful Big Brother figure. What those children wouldn't have given for one then.

ROBERT PROUDFOOT of Derby

When I was young my parents used to always play a song by the Alexander Bros called 'Nobody's Child'. The lines went, 'No mummy's kisses, no daddy's smiles, nobody wants me, I'm nobody's child.' At such a young age these lines used to haunt me and I would often cry myself to sleep.

That is why 'Suffer . . .' had quite an effect on me. It brought me back to when the thought of never seeing my parents again would terrify me. This is why 'Suffer . . .' is a special song to me; it makes me thankful of life and I suppose it wakes you up to the fact that you shouldn't take things for granted.

ANGIE J. LEWIS of Huddersfield, Yorkshire

I'm always close to tears any time I hear 'Suffer . . .' because it must be the most tragic reminder of the Moors Murders I've ever come across. I'm also forced to remember an occasion that I have never forgotten which happened a few years ago. I was travelling back from Manchester to Huddersfield after a day out, and I was listening to The Smiths on my walkman at the time. I was on the bus (the 364, which passes the bleak and desolate Saddleworth Moors where the unfortunate victims of Brady and Hindley were temporarily 'laid to rest'). I was falling asleep as 'Suffer Little Children' began to play. I could hear the words subconsciously as I was virtually dreaming by this time, when suddenly *someone who wasn't there* woke me up. I believe to this day that it was the ghost of one of the victims who aroused me from my rest, because it was the most eerie feeling I've ever had in my life. I wanted to run down the stairs and tell the bus driver to stop the bus but of course I couldn't. I'd got the idea into my head that whoever woke me up was trying to tell me where they were buried (because there still is, at this moment, some poor unfortunate child who's out there somewhere), but maybe I'm being hysterical. I do know, however, that I've never experienced anything like the sensation I had before or since.

HANNAH CORBETT of Retford, Nottinghamshire

'Suffer Little Children' was the fitting and poignant conclusion to an evening I spent in Sheffield some years ago after having seen Morrissey perform in the city. My brother Matt was a student there and after the show three of us adjourned to his place for a spot of Smiths and more than a spot of some fortified wine rubbish in order to retain the high. On went the first album as cans of lager were opened and the drunken singing came to a crescendo. What a night – watching grown men flail around the room to 'This Charming Man' only to slump in their chairs and shed tears on hearing 'Suffer Little Children'. Sober contemplation suddenly asserted itself, and eventually led into a discussion of Moz's supreme ability as a writer. A strange night, but ultimately a great one.

LIBBY of Walthamstow, London

Every Smiths song conjures up something in its own way, but I decided to choose 'Suffer Little Children' because of the emotions it stirred within me the very first time I listened to it.

Sufficiently enthused to buy the album on the strength of a *Top of the Pops* viewing of 'What Difference . . .', I had no idea just what an important influence on my life this band were to become. On first hearing, 'Suffer Little Children' moved me to tears as I sat rigid, a shiver raking my spine. No song had affected me in this startling way since my childhood days listening to 'Old Shep' by Jim Reeves. This time, of course, the tears were totally different; born of horrific realisation rather than youthful sentiment.

CLAUDIA HEIMAN of Cambridge, Massachusetts, USA

February 1994 – marked by the worst winter weather Boston had experienced in 50 years. The month I discovered Morrissey's music. I had just returned from a semester in London to my parents' house, to discover that virtually no friendships had survived the lengthy separation. I felt alienated at college and generally overwhelmed by a life dominated by stress, depression and loneliness. I felt trapped by the relentless desire for perfection and academic success and knew, deep down, that my true self was being suppressed.

Two o'clock one morning found me burning the midnight oil on an essay for college. The paper seemed to be going nowhere and suddenly I just stopped – desperate and panicky. Grabbing my walkman and a mixed Sandie Shaw/Smiths/Morrissey tape a good friend had made me for Valentine's Day, I left the house at a fast clip, all but running through the slumbering streets. The snow drifts and frozen puddles glimmered blue in a bleak and beautiful landscape.

When 'Suffer Little Children' came on I sank to the curbside, my heart heavy. Despite this, I sensed a tremendous release and couldn't stop shaking. Every nerve of my body suddenly *felt* everything – Morrissey's voice, full of tenderness and compassion, was one I instantly and instinctively trusted. Morrissey and the music somehow made it all right to simply sit on a curb in the dead of winter and be *alive* with passionate feelings. At that moment I saw my life at its most absurd and self destructive; the way in which my best qualities of responsibility and diligence had been twisted to the point where I could no longer express myself as myself. A young person aged 22 burdened already with a sense of world weariness.

I had never seen Manchester or the Moors or indeed met or seen anything more than a few pictures of Morrissey, yet I felt as if I'd known him forever. As if a spiritual twin had been discovered – one from whom I'd been separated at birth, only to reunite with later in life and find mutual qualities and outlooks on life. His voice seemed to emerge from within myself. 'Suffer Little Children' made me aware of my own mortality, my lost childhood and all the sadness and exhilaration I'd ever experienced. From a desolate childhood playground to saying goodbye to loved ones in London – all this fitted into a few bars of music. The epiphany was, to say the least, bittersweet and melancholic. I knew I had to someday meet the person who was the catalyst for my own development; who by the strength of a mere utterance could transport me out of myself to empathise with others' pain, thereby validating deep feelings and renewing my faith in the power of an individual voice to encourage and transform one's life.

Sweet And Tender Hooligan

IAIN KEY of Cheadle, Cheshire

An amazing night at The International in Manchester, dancing to this without having a clue what the hell it was. Later, watching The Primitives and meeting Tracey Tracey. I've still got the signed 'Stop Killing Me' T-shirt.

MADELAINE WEIDLER of Antwerp, Belgium

The first Smiths song I consciously listened to was 'Sweet And Tender Hooligan'. I was on a school trip to a region of Belgium of specific interest to my teachers – I've forgotten where; my interests lay elsewhere. A classmate sitting next to me on the coach handed me a walkman and invited me to listen to a song. This song. I was not allowed to hear more. But I was smitten, and I'd found a kindred soul whose voice rang true. And with that I ascended to lovely heights and was lost forever.

JULIE PLATT of London, SW2

I remember singing this while sitting out in the garden one summer's night. There were six of us I think. We'd got through a bucketful of homemade punch, and we had the record player on full volume with all the windows open so we could hear it

outside. 'In the midst of life we are in debt etc.' was sung particularly loudly.

That Joke Isn't Funny Anymore

IAIN KEY of Cheadle, Cheshire

I don't know why, but this reminds me of going to parties in Stretford and sleeping in cars or with fat women. A colleague's parents had moved and left the house to her, her sister and a female friend. Strange days . . .

DAVEY HUME of Liverpool

I grew up in a small, very narrow-minded northern town where being gay was almost unheard of. As a result, when I realised that I was attracted to my own sex, I felt incredibly isolated and very depressed. The only time lesbians or gays were ever mentioned there was as the butt of jokes: 'When you laugh about people who feel so very lonely, their only desire is to die.'

At school, both teachers and students would make jokes about 'queers who should be lined up against a wall and shot'. At the end of lessons I'd lock myself in the toilets and just cry. I never had the courage to tell these people about myself and they had no idea how much their comments hurt me. Now I've moved away from those awful times but one Smiths song still sums that experience up for me: 'That joke isn't funny anymore/It's too close to home and it's too near the bone/More than you'll ever know.'

ROBIN KENNEDY of Ayrshire, Scotland

The closing track of side one on The Smiths' finest LP, *Meat is Murder*, is one of the finest moments of the band on vinyl. Listening to this particular track I'm enveloped in Morrissey's melancholia but such feelings aren't allowed to wander free – they are subtly restrained through the wonderful waltz-time music put together by Marr.

This particular track brings back the memory of myself at fifteen standing transfixed in the middle of my bedroom, stunned at the sheer beauty and emotion of the track. For me, the final refrain of the song, as Morrissey wails, 'I've seen this happen in other people's lives and now it's happening in mine,' amidst crashing cymbals and drum rolls is extremely moving. The song stands the test of time because it's balanced perfectly between unrestrained sadness and regimented music.

There Is A Light That Never Goes Out

JO COOPER of Hampstead, London

In August last year, my niece Alex and her boyfriend John came over from Belfast for a short holiday. Never having met John before, I relished the opportunity to show off my assorted Smiths memorabilia and photographs. These days, they make only sporadic appearances from the dark corners of the drawers and cupboards in which they lurk. Afterwards, I left the photo albums on the table in the front room, not quite finding the energy or inclination to pack them away. Some days later, my mother visited as I was off work sick. In daughterly fashion, I headed through to the kitchen to make tea, forgetting that the albums lay unguarded at her elbow. As the kettle boiled, her comments drifted through the open doorway.

'Oh, look at you and Johnny Marr.'

'Wasn't your hair different then?'

She then came through to the kitchen clutching a long-forgotten snap. I was demure, long-haired and seventeen. I didn't want to look at that photograph.

It showed a room in the Britannia Hotel, Manchester. July 1986. I had no job and no money but was in the city to see The Smiths in concert. My ex-boyfriend had paid for my stay at the Britannia, and even though I felt uncomfortable and awkward at being in his debt, it had seemed worth it to see the band. But shortly after that photograph was taken, I was being dragged about the room by my hair and forced to watch him inject himself with speed under the (very real) threat of further violence.

Later, much later, I somehow found my frightened, confused way to the hotel bar where the band (minus Morrissey) were drinking. I approached Johnny, struck suddenly by the realisation that I'd never see The Smiths again. We chatted for an hour about unimportant things while I tried to straighten myself with several vodkas. Ruth Polsky, The Smiths' American promoter, joined us as we talked, drank and took photos.

I never did see the band together again. Salford University that July evening was my 42nd Smiths gig, and number 43 would never arrive. My swansong. Some months later, I read that Ruth Polsky had died in a freak accident in New York. To this day, 'There Is A Light . . .' sparks memories of that crazy night. Memories of Johnny, of Ruth, of the Britannia Hotel, Manchester and the closing episode of one part of my life.

MARTIN COOPER of Glasgow

They thought we were having sex and didn't like it. We *were* having sex and I bloody well *did* like it. Banned from seeing her I had to concoct elaborate excuses or sneak out, slyly taking the car keys with me. Once in the car and speeding down back lanes a tape would be slapped on. A good driving one: 'There Is A Light . . .' It would never last. I was too young; it was a futile teenage crush; lust is not love. Eight years later and we're still married.

NICK KING of Nottingham

The closing months of 1986 found me on a Youth Training Scheme to which I would travel, daily, by bus. Each morning I would drool over a particularly gorgeous fellow passenger who never, it seemed, sat anywhere near me. At last the morning arrived when the bus was full and I found myself sharing the back seat with the object of my sexual desire. The heartbeat and macabre lines of 'There Is A Light . . .' came to mind: to die by her side would indeed have been a pleasure and a privilege. With so much flying glass the scene would've been pretty gory, but at least I'd have finally been able to enjoy the pleasure of exchanging bodily fluids with someone for the very first time . . .

TON DE VRIES of Rotterdam, Holland

I studied economics and had almost finished the course. But my final thesis was killing me – constant depression led to the suicidal thoughts I thought had left my mind for ever. I decided not to complete that thesis for the transportation company. I visited the boss of the company and told him I was quitting. He, along with my professor, vainly attempted to convince me otherwise, but my mind was set.

I called a girlfriend, feeling free as a bird. When I arrived at her house 'There Is A Light . . .' was playing. She really helped me, impressing upon me that my studies *were* important. Two days later, I began a new thesis, about the nineteenth-century economists W. S. Jevons and Leon Walras. Soon I was reading old books in German, French and English as well as love letters. I lived again and graduated one year after that day. Since then, every time I hear this song I relive that strange day and thank the girl for her inspiration.

Ms NICK BURTON of Braunstone Town, Leicester

The song evokes memories of my first visit to Coventry, going to see The Primitives at the Tic Toc club. The journey from Leicester to Coventry is via the 21-mile M69 built specifically for this route (i.e. it doesn't go anywhere else). Travelling along this short, straight road gave me a Kerouacian sense of purpose – I felt on the road, as it were, as if life finally had meaning. I didn't really care where I was heading, as long as it was away from the oppressive suburbia that had framed my life since the day I was born. 'Take me anywhere, I don't care, I don't care . . .' I now remember the evening for the blossoming of a beautiful romance. Not just between myself and a whole subculture. A whole new way of life that I understood and related to the moment I set eyes on it.

GRAHAM COLEMAN of Hampstead, London

New Year's Eve '86 – five of us were renting a flat in north London and another five friends were staying the night. At pub closing-time someone suggested making for Trafalgar Square to join the festivities. Having experienced this hell at first hand before, I tried to talk them out of it. I met with glassy-eyed contempt as they entered the fray. My girlfriend pleaded with me to join in the 'fun' but no, I was the immovable object. Furthermore, I was in possession of four cans of beer and had been advised by a friendly policeman that they could not be taken in on grounds that they could be used as lethal weapons. Unwilling to jettison such a valuable cargo I returned to the flat in reflective mood . . . surely if I was a normal, sociable human being I'd jump at the chance to be crushed by thousands of sweaty morons bellowing in my ears and vomiting on my shoes?

Now, this was the evening that Peel's 'Festive Fifty' came to its conclusion. Back home I listened to the last few tracks and drank the beer and waited for the others to return, which they did, in dribs and drabs mostly. I greeted them with the news that 'There Is A Light . . .' had claimed top spot. My girlfriend, meanwhile, had accepted a lift from a drunken maniac who (she soon realised) had no intention of taking her in the agreed direction. Baling out at some traffic lights she decided to walk home despite her exiguous knowledge of London geography. A rather ugly scene developed on her late arrival which need not be resurrected here. Offering an 'olive branch', I informed her of the big news – that The Smiths had been number one. I forget her precise words, but have never again been tempted to insert pop trivia into emotionally charged situations . . .

FIONA of Stoke-on-Trent, Staffs

I still wonder whatever possessed me to sign away an entire summer working for Camp America. Wanderlust, I suppose. I found myself marooned in the remote heart of West Virginia, on a children's summer camp half an hour's drive from the nearest signs of civilisation. Even getting that far was problematic; we had first to commandeer one of the tatty, rattling, yellow school buses which might have come straight from the set of *The Waltons*. And yet I recall the experience with great fondness. After all, the alternative would have been to spend summer in murky old England, perhaps returning to my previous employment in a bookshop.

Among those Blue Ridge mountains, treasured afternoons away from work were often spent at the poolside, offering our lily-white limbs to the sun's rays. The lifeguard, Geoff, soon became a source of amusement to us Brits abroad. Muscles bulging and rippling on his deep brown torso, he'd parade, pose and prowl his way around the swimming pool, hungry, leering eyes concealed behind mirrored sunshades.

To our astonishment, the preening Narcissus displayed commendable taste in music when 'There Is A Light . . .' was to be heard amidst his otherwise loathsome collection of AOR. Surrounded by the Blue Ridge mountains, lush green trees and gently fluttering Union flags, I was immediately transported back to my beloved (if rain-lashed) England.

SEAN HOSKINS of Heamoor, Cornwall

In the centre of Cardiff (where I'm studying), there is a light at the top of a huge office block which can be seen for miles around. In the minds of a friend and myself, this is the 'light that never goes out' since it radiates warmth and security and can always be relied upon.

At a party in Bristol, I was given a lift home by a friend of a friend. Before three minutes of the hour-long journey had elapsed, I realised that my chauffeur was a snooty madam who found it distasteful being associated with low-class persons such as me. A nightmare trip. The longest hour . . . I remember spotting the light as we entered Cardiff and reciting to myself the lines of the song: 'If a double-decker bus, crashes into us/To die by your side . . . would be the worst possible way to die.'

CHRIS NANOS of Toronto, Canada

My friend and I would sometimes go on road trips. Road trips are the best. We would head for places which were distant enough but still accessible from Toronto. We'd drive to out-of-town record stores, to Fairmount in Indiana (James Dean's hometown) and to Niagara Falls. The best trips were often those without any predetermined destination. We would just go. Drive. But that was long ago and I guess we just got tired of driving together. Whatever.

The music we'd play in the car was the greatest. One song we played over and over was 'There Is A Light . . .' by The Smiths. The lines of that song were so creepy, hearing them as we cruised those highways and byways laced with ten ton trucks. 'And if a double-decker bus, crashes into us/To die by your side, such a heavenly way to die . . .' These words would vibrate inside the car and his hands would shake on the wheel and I felt that wherever he was going to take that car I would have gone.

I really hated to hear that song ending, just as I hated coming home from road trips. For a day or two I'd feel something that was actually the opposite of homesickness. I guess it was post-vacation blues. I would be frustrated and almost sick to the stomach. It was like I just wanted to go out and stay out. Whatever. Bret Easton Ellis had it right in *Less Than Zero*.

'Where are we going?'
'I don't know . . . just driving.'
'But this road doesn't go anyplace . . .'
'That doesn't matter.'
'What does?'
'Just that we're on it, dude.'

It's great when a band on the radio, a band you've never met, a group of people who don't even know you exist, can write and produce a song which is so uncannily YOU. If anyone wanted to know anything about me, all they'd need to do would be to listen to that song.

CRAIG STAFF of Crick, Northamptonshire

Summer's promise had faded, and as I gazed out of the car window my eyes followed the weakening rays of sunlight as they slanted across the fields. We dropped David at his home – a farmhouse steeped in the rustic atmosphere of the Leicestershire countryside. The car struggled back up the farmyard driveway and on to the main road and Annabelle and myself began our homeward journey.

We were halfway through our A levels, and as I surveyed the darkening landscape I wondered if the others were feeling as restless as I was. Annabelle seemed preoccupied as she stared silently at the road ahead being swiftly gobbled up. Sadly, my knowledge of her amounted to very little. Her voice broke the silence. 'This road we're driving along used to be a runway.' The long, black strip of tarmac was reaching out for a distant horizon. I imagined planeloads of passengers touching down upon this very spot; anxious, excited people being drawn upwards into a gaping sky. Take me anywhere, I don't care, I don't care . . .

I found myself asking Annabelle if she'd heard a song entitled 'There Is A Light . . .' by The Smiths. She hadn't, which both relieved and disappointed me since I considered it a most wonderful love song. Almost despite myself, I began describing the song in intricate detail. It was as if her telling me about the runway was somehow a question and demanded a response, an answer.

SAM HAMPSON of Shrewsbury, Shropshire

It was 1986 and I was a sweet, naïve creature, all of sixteen years old and just starting out in the school sixth form. I met a rather luscious university student at a party one night and suddenly my life was turned upside-down. This was the one! I proceeded to move heaven and earth to organise a date with him, and succeeded.

Anyway, to cut a long story short, my plans of everlasting love were thwarted. He returned to university after getting off with someone else (I cried for weeks), and that was that. We only had a couple of dates, but I was devastated. At this time, the main tape that was being played in our sixth form centre (much to the dismay of the secretarial students around at the same time) was *The Queen is Dead*. As well as listening to this at school, it was a fave album to play in my room at home. During this time of woe brought on by the rejection of my luscious friend, I suddenly became aware of a song that must have been definitely written for me. 'There Is A Light That Never Goes Out' was that song. In a bizarre way, it served as a kind of comforter to me in those dark times of teen love gone terribly wrong. I still think of that using pig to this day when I hear that song. How sad that such a pretty song should be placed in history with such a naïve time. But then that was part of the charm of this particular band. They summed up situations that were felt in the hearts of us all. And still do so to this day.

NEIL ASHMORE of Stockport, Cheshire

The first woman I became very attracted to had left my place of work some eighteen months previously, but I always hoped to see her again someday. The dreamed-for meeting eventually took place one dark evening just prior to Christmas '90 in the doorway of my local Iceland supermarket. It amounted to little more than polite 'Hello's before we went our separate ways. Travelling home by train later that day I heard 'There Is A Light . . .' for the very first time and it brought the proverbial lump to my throat. The 'darkened underpass' or the doorway of a foodstore – I guess it's all the same.

ANDREW TAYLOR of Bootle, Liverpool

A gorgeous reminder of the halcyon days of summer '86 and the first 'serious' relationship I had entered into. The sun always seemed to be shining as Ruth and I drove around in her bottle-green MG Midget, roof down, and *The Queen is Dead* blasting from the car stereo. The quiet lanes of Ormskirk and Melling had probably never seen the likes of it before! Two young lovers speeding around so fast with the songs of The Smiths trailing in their heady wake. This song seemed so apt to the way we felt at that time. We'd wander into the local pub, The Bootle Arms in Melling, humming the song and discussing over drinks what a wonderful time we were having with one another.

SOPHIE LEGENCHE of Neuville-Sur-Oise, France

This one I remember precisely. It was December 1990. 'Take me out tonight/Because I want to see people and I want to see lights.' Of course I'd have loved that on this cold Saturday night as I was walking on my own in the crowded streets of Paris which was already showing off its Christmas dress. 'The city which doesn't sleep' so they say. Well, not for me because that night my light was only flickering and I was heading nowhere but towards my bed.

All Men Have Secrets

KEN HOLMES of Lincoln

The radio was on in the corner of the room, but I wasn't really paying much attention to it. All of a sudden 'There Is A Light That Never Goes Out' began to play. At the time the song was entirely new to me, and I didn't know a thing about The Smiths, but it made such an impression that I knew there and then that I had to get hold of everything they'd ever recorded.

Before that I'd never taken much of an interest in music, but about a minute into the song I knew I had to tape it, or at least try to. I rushed into my sister's room where there was a radio cassette recorder, turned it on, and hurriedly tried to find the right station, expecting the song to finish at any moment. Luckily I wasn't long in finding it, so snatching up a blank tape I slammed it into the machine and pressed the record button.

I actually managed to get just the last bit, but that didn't matter. A short time later I bought my first Smiths tape.

CHERYL KRUNKROSKI of Franklin Park, New Jersey, USA

Some years ago, before his untimely death, my love and I would spend hours driving at night oblivious to the real world. With the car stereo blasting our favourite tunes, we never wanted to part and say goodnight. To have died side by side when our love was in full bloom would have been pure heaven. We shared a Patti Smith song, 'Dancing Barefoot'. She chants, 'Oh God, I fell for you,' and that line enters my mind every time I hear Johnny Marr's string arrangement.

ALEX GREEN of Uddingston, Lanarkshire

Initially, I hated The Smiths, but have found over the years that I was not the only one to undergo conversion. I'm really glad those first impressions didn't last. The turning point came in the summertime of 1984.

Two o'clock in the morning, sitting on a veranda in a
Tenerife hotel. There's Wullie Bowman and myself and Paul
Somerset from Farnham, Surrey – just one of the legion of
people we met that fortnight. Inside, the girls are demolishing
what's left of two bottles of Blue Label vodka. Paul asked us to
listen to The Smiths – 'This band are what living is all about.'
His request, although met with apprehension, didn't really beg
dissent. This *was* his balcony, after all. Two hours later, both
Wullie and myself were mesmerised, shattered, heartbroken –
we'd cried solid. Paul, thank you for changing my life.

We returned to Scotland and began the crusade, telling everyone about the band. No one had really heard of them, but
things were about to change! We forced records upon malleable
DJs and before long every disco would be listening to 'This
Charming Man'. Soon, the floors were mobbed. Not surprisingly, the Bruce Springsteen fans moaned loud and long: tough
shit, Brucie fans, The Smiths had hit town in a very big way.
The local butchers were no less angry as more and more people
became vegetarian. Tough shit, butchers.

To this day I remain vegetarian. To this day, I ask for The
Smiths records to be played wherever I go. To this day, the DJs
still play them. To this day, I'm still not sure where exactly to
find the light that never goes out. But searching is a lot of fun.

MARIAN COLE of Brooklyn, New York, USA

I finally got to meet Morrissey in spring '94 when he did an in-
store record signing here in New York. While waiting in line, I
racked my brains trying to figure out what to say and finally
came up with 'Thank you'. What else is there to say really? Still,
I wish I'd thought to thank him specifically for this song – the
most beautiful and heartbreaking ever. I think of 'the light that
never goes out' as my love for Morrissey, I guess. I could never,
ever feel entirely alone in the world as long as he is around and
his records remain. When I met him and he hugged me (swoon!)

199

it was all I could do to stop myself from saying, 'And if a double decker bus crashes into us . . .'

LAURENCE HUGHES of Tufnell Park, London

My most recent vivid memory is as follows. It's from this year. At the time I happened to be hurtling along a motorway in Shropshire at about 80mph. (Funny, my associations all seem to be about travel.) We had The Smiths playing on the cassette machine as usual – my all time favourite track, 'There Is A Light That Never Goes Out'. As Marr's guitar crashed and jangled and Morrissey crooned away, I gazed out of the window (I wasn't driving!) to see the Wrekin – the great conical extinct volcano with an Iron Age fort on the summit that broods over the River Severn – illuminated in a wonderful silvery glow by a huge full moon. An incredibly strong sense of timelessness came over me. It was one of those moments, again. And what it said to me was, OK, it's the best part of a decade now since they split up, and Morrissey's showing signs of middle-age spread in every sense (then, aren't we all?), but things that really matter *last*.

The songs are still there – there for ever – and they'll be an endless source of 'special memories' for us, and for generations to come.

MIKE CAMPBELL of Giffnock, Glasgow

After several years of thankless, fruitless labour in the retail trade, I decided to try and kickstart my life by disappearing to America for a while. I have family (and a large extended family) just outside Los Angeles, so in true Dick Whittington style I packed my things into the proverbial red spotted handkerchief and headed west in January of 1991. The easiest way to acquire an American visa is to educate oneself – or at least pretend to do so. So I duly enrolled at Orange Coast College on the

Monday following my arrival. I felt like a bit of an oddity which was unsurprising given that I was the only Scottish student among 28,000 prospective graduates. My peers, while being extremely welcoming and friendly, were often just plain baffled by Scottish standard English.

In the weeks and months that passed I developed a routine for my days at college. I would wander round to the Arco petrol station about an hour before my class and have a chat with Rob, the young attendant. Rob had, at first, like everyone else, been floundering with the way I spoke. Trying to buy twenty Marlboro Lights seemed like a major operation but through a combination of over-enunciated phrases and sign language the necessary nicotine would be purchased.

Rob was just as fascinated with the fact that people really *did* eat fish and chips from newspaper in Britain as I was with the fact that drinking a beer in public would inevitably incur the wrath of the Orange County Police Department. I learned a lot about Californian culture from these lazy afternoon chats and came to enjoy them immensely.

One afternoon in June I walked round to class via the Arco station as usual. Sighting Rob, I gave him a wave, but for some reason there was no smile or cheery acknowledgement. Something was quite definitely amiss. It transpired that on the previous evening, Rob and his friend Denise had travelled up to LA to see Morrissey performing at the Forum. With the concert over they had returned to Huntington Beach, where Denise had dropped Rob at home before continuing onwards. She never arrived home. They found her car at the junction of Bear Street and Bristol Street which was less than a mile from the house in which I was staying. She had simply vanished and the police had placed the blame for her disappearance squarely on Rob's shoulders. Evidently they had questioned him all night and had really terrified the poor guy. What can you say to someone who has been through this sort of ordeal? He had lost on both counts: his friend was missing and he was on the receiving end of some undoubtedly harrowing treatment for it.

Standing in the baking heat of that California afternoon and unable to proffer any meaningful words of support other than 'I'm sorry' left me feeling empty and bitter. How could this have happened to such a decent, ordinary guy? I felt like screaming, but somehow even that would have been redundant. Denise's family put up a massive white poster on the side of a hotel next to the spot where her car was found, appealing for information. I used to pass it on a regular basis but no matter how many times I saw it, it never ever became familiar. A chill overcame me each and every time and I wished and wished she would just turn up so that, if nothing else, Rob would be fully exonerated. Sadly though, she never did.

That September I returned to Scotland to attend university in Glasgow. As things returned to normal and I settled back into my routine, I would often think of Denise and that poster. In my mind's eye it continued to flutter in the gentle Santa Ana winds, its dust streaked by freak showers leaving it dirty and tattered as if besmirching the fake panstick of Tinseltown.

I have returned several times since then, the most recent visit being in September 1994 when the poster, for the first time, was down: gone with it the hope of ever seeing Denise alive again. The details are unnecessary but her body had been found. Now when I hear 'There Is A Light . . .' I think of her family and wonder if, for them, the light burns still.

These Things Take Time

TIM CROUCH of London, NW5

I had a very good friend who 'quite liked' Morrissey. Well, that wouldn't do, so I foisted three albums upon him, *Louder Than Bombs* being among them. The ploy, for once, worked. He was hooked. We went through a fair amount together and discovered a lot about ourselves. One afternoon we were in my bedroom, talking. We got some beers, for he was a big fan of Directors bitter, and found ourselves discussing life, the universe and Joanna, who featured regularly in such conversations. *Louder Than Bombs* provided the ideal musical backdrop. I taught him how to 'shotgun' a can of beer, which we did a couple of times before devouring two raw quiches. 'These Things Take Time' coincided with a lull in our therapeutic ramblings and it dawned on us that *this* was one of those 'alcoholic afternoons' about which Morrissey was singing. We were living the record. After that, the song was first on every tape we made and became a 'must' on such occasions.

NORMAN CUMMINS of Govan, Glasgow

My alcoholic afternoons. Finishing work early on a Friday and, for a year and a half without fail, making straight for RGs in Queen Street, there to drink vast quantities of draught

Budweiser. Someone would always be sent to Burger King at teatime to smuggle cheeseburgers back into the pub. After that, my memory becomes hazy . . . Great days.

JON SCOTT of Putney, London

Never has a title been more apt. I am cycling up one side of the Grimsel Pass, a 1,500 metre climb in the shadow-ridden Swiss Alps, and am listening to *Hatful of Hollow*. It is my album of the trip, the dozen or so songs which will later help me to re-member that widened perspective I curiously think I have when out of breath and surrounded by such ominous beauty.

Perhaps it's not so curious. This particular song stubbornly allies itself to my lonely ascent of the Grimsel Pass at dusk. I rewind as soon as it finishes; I'm not sure I'll reach the summit without it. I look down at the twenty hairpin bends I have con-quered so far. I can see my friend Greg, very small, three or four behind me. He is climbing without The Smiths.

The odd car scurries past, eager to find trees and grass once more. It is a strange mixture; my legs are in agony, while my head is euphoric – but they seem to complement each other. I reach the top, and am immediately nostalgic for the climb, con-scious of having had 'the moment' of the tour. The setting sun is an unwanted reward for my pains, and I am envious of Greg, who still has ten minutes to go. I press STOP on my walkman, have a beer in a wooden roadside shack and talk to some other cyclists about gear ratios.

This Charming Man

GRAHAM COLEMAN of Hampstead, London

August 1992. I visited a friend in Folkestone while he was teaching English to foreign students at a summer school. There was a disco one night and when this was played (it had just been re-released) it emptied the dancefloor of Europe's teenagers in seconds. We were the only two left, painfully aware that the verdict of the youthful, international jury was 'what a pair of sad old tossers'.

DEAN AINSCOUGH of Edenvale, South Africa

To many he was known as Steven; to others, Mr Ainscough; to my friends, Uncle Steve, but to me he was just Dad. As with most families, we had our share of problems. Arguments and fights were commonplace until my parents finally divorced in 1989. I lost touch with Dad after that and it wasn't until two years later that I began seeing him again. By that time, he had made a new life for himself and I was proud of him for doing so. We got along famously, but after a year or so he suddenly went downhill. His girlfriend left him and he lost his job. He began to drink excessively and because of this I once again kept my distance. Whether this was the right thing to do has troubled me ever since. Whenever it seemed as though he was getting back on his feet, something would invariably come along and knock him down again. 'A manic depressive' someone called him. Well, whatever – I guess he'd just had enough of this life and its cruelty because he committed suicide not long after that.

I'd like to dedicate 'This Charming Man' to the memory of a man who certainly was. Charming, witty, understanding and generous. Dad.

ROB MARSHALL of Wood Green, London

A cold February evening, 1984. I recall sitting in the bath contemplating life, death and whether or not to drown the plastic duck when from the bowels of a battered wireless issued a call to arms and 'a punctured bicycle on a hillside desolate'. A watershed. For once in my puny life I'd been in the right place at the right time. My next five years were to be measured out in songs, quiffs and scrawled postcards from Smiths fans in Great Yarmouth. Then one sunny day in 1843 it all came to an end: no new songs to cling to – merely a floundering quiff to mark the spot. The postcards still arrived, albeit sporadically now, but it wasn't the same somehow. It really did seem the most propitious of times to stop the world and clamber off (with a gentle persuasive push from Mother?). But life went on, and still does. The scratched Rough Trade vinyl remains very much part of the furniture, making its weekly appearance in much the same way as the milkman. Or any time when the past creeps up on me while watching *Brookside*.

Last year I committed the crime of selling my entire collection of *Smiths Indeed* for the less-than-princely sum of five pints of lager. What would have been deemed a heinous offence in the halcyon days of '84 still jarred, but I was in dire need of alcoholic refreshment. The spotty purchaser of said fanzines enquired as to whether Smiths tracks still haunted my gramophone. I nodded politely, but had not the heart to tell him that them was rotten days. Ah, but then again, where would I be without the very lifeblood of misery coursing through my self-indulgent veins? As Jean Rhys succinctly commented, '. . . and then it became a part of me and I would have missed it had it gone.'

When all's said and done, when the cat's been kicked out and Melvyn Bragg is searching for the perfect epitaph, The Smiths were only a pop group, weren't they? Oh no . . .

CALUM McGILP of Studland, Dorset

Takes me back to my early-morning milkround days. Pushing the milk trolley up and down the steep streets and bleary-eyed customers emerging from their doorways without a stitch to wear. Perhaps the band should've used a picture of Cary Grant on the sleeve.

SARAH BRADBURY of New Moston, Manchester

Outside, the rain poured on humdrum Manchester, but Café Pop, with its 1960s style interior and old music posters, was alive.

Jenny and I decided to stick 'This Charming Man' on the jukebox – sometimes the best ideas needn't be all that new or original! The scene might've been culled from a Smiths video – the miserable businessman in the corner suddenly transformed himself into Morrissey, flouncing around and singing. All he needed was a quiff and a spray of gladioli. Meanwhile, service was postponed for a full three minutes as the waiters and wait-resses danced to this wonderful song.

There was a joyous sense of Manchester celebrating its own – just for once. The Smiths were, are and surely always will be our town's greatest triumph. Even George Best was only an 'adopted' Manc!

All Men Have Secrets

PATRICK CLAEYS of Blankenberge, Belgium

The beginnings of my Smiths addiction. After hearing this magical song on *Top of the Pops* in '83 (27 November), I hurried to a local record shop. Inevitably they had to order me a copy and surprisingly, it turned out to be the New York mix which is quite collectable now.

JOAN CANAL OLIVERAS of Manresa, Spain

I can still see this guy Dave, from London, who was staying at the hotel in which I worked as a receptionist in a Spanish coastal resort. He wore Joy Division and Smiths T-shirts all the time and one day we started talking music. 'Do you know "This Charming Man"?' he asked. 'You must.' And he handed me the complete Smiths which he'd taped at home so as not to be too far from them on his holidays. 'Don't worry – I can tape it again. If you like The Smiths, it's OK.' For the rest of his visit, I devoted myself to showing him round my favourite bars and places in town. We would go out drinking lots of beer and talking of our lives for hours on end.

PHILL GATENBY of Moston, Manchester

For several years I was a contributor to a football fanzine entitled *Blue Print* which covered the pains and strains of Manchester City FC. I always like to top off my pieces with a Smiths song as the heading. For example, we once signed a player named Bill Williams who appeared for 70-odd minutes before being substituted and never seen again. His farewell carried the heading, 'Williams, It Was Really Nothing.'

When *Blue Print* wound up, I decided to go ahead and produce a fanzine of my own. Choosing the name was proving difficult until I thought of the obvious – Smiths titles! Of course, there was no contest. The first song I owned was the seven-inch single 'This Charming Man' and it remains a favourite even now. So I am now the editor of *This Charming Fan* and still searching for song titles to lead the articles.

Ms NICK BURTON of Braunstone Town, Leicester

Cheap lager, crying with Gazza in the World Cup and driving round the M25 in a classic car looking for an acid house party.

CRAIG FINNEY of Reading, Berkshire

Potting sheds and petunias, rather than *Top of the Pops* and gladioli. Between my second and third years at university, I landed a summer job as a maintenance gardener in Regent's Park, London. The choice lay between that and a processed-meat factory, and the prospect of fresh air and an extra 30p per hour was enough to sway my decision in favour of the outdoor life. As things turned out, nature chucked in a decent tan as a bonus, the summer of '84 being very long and (perhaps too!) hot.

There, brush and hoe in hand, I communed happily with nature for three carefree months. Roaming the lawns and rambling through the bushes, I made friends with the squirrels and enemies of canoodling lovers under blue summer skies. I fell hopelessly in love with the ice-cream girl from Bulgaria but received nothing in return save for double dollops of rum 'n' raisin. And The Smiths played on ... when Leonard wasn't around.

Leonard had been a gardener for hundreds of years. I had no doubt that his gnarled hands had lovingly tended the flowers and plants of the Garden of Eden. He was probably more pissed off than God over the whole apple business. Leonard was my teacher and mentor, and a better teacher and mentor I could not have wished for. Aside from his wife Babs, Leonard's chief loves in life were Dulwich Hamlet FC, purple petunias and the rich aroma of fresh horse manure. His flat cap and collarless shirt hinted at direct lineage from the esteemed kitchen gardeners of Victorian England. For him, the world (my world) of books and exams and The Smiths was as remote and foreign as the giant cactus or the eucalyptus tree. His attitude to my university education sometimes bordered on the cap-doffing servitude of those aforementioned antecedents. It would have come as no shock whatsoever had he addressed me as 'guv'nor'. In a few short weeks, I grew to love him.

Which gave rise to a quandary: my habit, during the first few weeks was to eat lunch (always ice-cream) while lounging on the grass outside the shed which served as our headquarters. There, for an hour, I would close my eyes and dream of Tasha with every lick of chocolate chip. The Smiths' debut album, plus a few other odds and sods, comprised the tape which filled perfectly my hour-long break. It was perfect. Leonard, meantime, sat quietly in the shade of the shed eating cheese sandwiches and reading the *Daily Express*.

Before long I realised several things – that I wasn't going to get any browner, that I could listen to The Smiths *any* time, and that here was an old man whom I increasingly liked and wanted to know better. I started lunching indoors, which seemed to please him.

We became great friends. One day he asked me about the music – my liking for which both intrigued and baffled him. How the hell does one even begin to explain The Smiths to an old man like Leonard? I played him 'This Charming Man' which seemed entirely appropriate. Of course it meant nothing to him, but then that wasn't really the point. It was just meant.

JENNIFER BRUNDAGE of San Jose, California, USA

Completely perfect and giddy. Three things, really – a rainy, foggy winter in San Francisco, the video on which they performed the song (and noting that Morrissey's haircut seemed much more clumsy then, with bits shaved too close) and being struck by the similarity of the line 'leather runs smooth . . .' to one which appears in 'That Joke Isn't Funny Anymore'.

MIKE DOWD of Salford, Manchester

There is always that one household, remembered fondly from the necessity of our youth, where through favour or circumstance a more liberal and relaxed regime was operated than in most homes. A 'safe house', where dark midweek evenings could be languished through, fed by endless cups of tea, cigarettes, guitar practice and extravagant dreams. A schoolfriend occupied just such a domain, where the boom of loud music emitting from an aged stereogram could invariably be heard, its lid heavy with discarded coffee mugs and the laurels of his record collection.

Until, that is, the riptide of rumour we had so steadfastly and sceptically ignored from more fashionable Hacienda-going friends proved itself to be gloriously true. 'This Charming Man' burst from the television one Friday evening during *The Tube* and things would never be quite the same again.

My friend's elder brother, already a fledgling convert and soon to embrace fanaticism, was then in educational exile at Leeds Polytechnic. His coming to terms with higher (?) education coincided with the tarnishing and/or dissolution of previous musical heroes, but this did not mean that the longed-for transfusion of fresh blood would be accepted without full medical check. Looking back, there can have been little doubt that The Smiths would pass any examination going. Those autumn and winter evenings in the back downstairs room continued, weekends in particular being memorable for the strains of 'This Charming Man', 'Accept Yourself', 'Jeane', et al., issuing forth from the bathroom where our mentor would luxuriate in his homecoming ablutions for hours on end.

All Men Have Secrets

NICKY BRAIN of Tallahassee, Florida, USA

In September 1984 I attended Macclesfield College. The new term brought with it an abundance of new faces, myself included, many of whom later went on to become good friends.

On one particular afternoon while my friend Janet and I were dithering about whether to show up for a maths lecture or not, we bumped into a couple of guys quite obviously in the throes of a similar dilemma. We got talking and the outcome was overwhelming agreement that we should ditch our respective classes in favour of a jaunt up to the Peak District in Charlie's car.

When I say Charlie's car, I really mean *Charlie's car*. Everyone at the college was familiar with it. Latterly, a sighting of the rustbucket white Fiesta before 5 p.m. could mean only one thing – Charlie was skiving yet another class. Even the lecturers came to recognise it. When they saw us trundling past, I often wondered what they must have thought of us, especially as Charlie and his mate were retaking their A levels and had blown last year's attempt as a result of similar bouts of wanderlust.

It was the consensus that sunny late afternoon that we would go to the Cat and Fiddle, a pub which has the honour of being the highest boozer in England, so they say. It sits in the middle of nowhere which, I assure you, was the perfect substitute for an overcrowded, underwhelming classroom back at Macc College.

The car juddered and spluttered its way up the hills as the four of us made slightly awkward conversation. Despite a few pregnant pauses it was clear to me that we did all have something in common as the lot of us were dressed head to foot in black even though it was a sweltering day. Back then this could mean only one thing – you were into The Smiths or Depeche Mode. Given that Charlie's mate had a quiff like an anvil, I decided to broach the sometimes thorny issue of musical taste. By some miraculous chance, my questions and prospective opinions were interrrupted by the sparkling opening chimes of 'This Charming Man'.

Now, I don't know if any of you have ever car-danced before but if you have then I'll wager it wasn't at 50 mph in a mobile death trap with two complete strangers. You really should try it on those occasions when the chat is running a bit dry. It most certainly breaks the ice. With arms flailing, voices wailing and limbs out of windows we moshed about the Fiesta caring about nothing other than how Moz-like we could sound. The car bunny-hopped onwards in the general direction of Buxton as cyclists and hill walkers alike scattered in our path. This felt like the beginning of something quite special as we commenced what was to become the first of many legendary alcoholic afternoons.

Needless to say, I had made a good call regarding which band everyone liked and you could safely say that it was the music of The Smiths which cemented our friendship. Anthony, Charlie's mate, was not averse to comparing Morrissey with God. His religion really was The Smiths. At six foot three, with blue eyes and that big loaf of hair, Anthony was a lovely looking guy. He was never big-headed about it though, except perhaps in a hair sense of course! He and I were soon to become flirty friends. We loved going swimming in Wilmslow together – him to avoid lectures and me out of curiosity to see what he looked like with a flattened quiff. I loved his company and especially his wry sense of humour. In fact Janet and I loved both the boys' company and they ours but as is sadly so often the case, the academic year came and went and our contact gradually dwindled. I haven't been back to Macclesfield for some time. I hear Anthony still lives there and he's married now – he's probably got a string of little Tonys with mini-quiffs in tow. I do hope that I'll meet up with him again some time but until I do I've only to hear 'This Charming Man' and in my mind's eye I can see him writhing on the passenger seat of Charlie's car. Eleven years on, I still remember that Charlie was crazy about Janet and I wonder if anything ever came of that almost as often as I think of Tony. That charming man.

All Men Have Secrets

KERRI SHARP of Camberwell, London

Working my way through film school often meant being cheap labour for employers of dubious integrity: in restaurants, mostly. I found myself, one evening in the mid-eighties, elbow deep in a sink full of chicken carcasses ('scrunt' duty) for a crêperie in the King's Road. Intestinal garbage of 'nam-like proportions. Horror spasm abyss.

Relief came in the form of two chirpy lads from Liverpool (Richie Johnstone and Gary Bleasdale – nephew of Alan and one of Harry Enfield's 'Scousers'), who worked the kitchens with me and who, also like me, loathed the gaff's mincing proprietor who wouldn't let us work the floor because we 'had accents'.

By the end of our shift, the clubs were nearly closed and our aprons were covered in gunk. And the three of us would bemoan our fate, thrust sticks of celery and carrots deep into our back pockets, exaggerate to maximum extent those Liverpool accents, prance about in an affected manner and sing, 'Oh I'd go out tonight, but I haven't got a stitch to wear . . .'

This Night Has Opened My Eyes

MIKE DOWD of Salford, Manchester

So it is then, that I alighted a number 12 bus at Pendleton Church, Salford, and walked down Broughton Road – the morning sky misty black and sagging like old tarpaulin. Past the Albert Finney shop on the corner of Lissadel Street and Cromwell Road, its 'DSS Estimates' freshly whitewashed in the window. A sign of the (new) times. Then onward along Gerald Road and Blandford Road, sleek seal pavements and red raddled terraces looking the epitome of 'Beesley Street'. And finally Conniston Street's cobbles led me to the gates of Irwell Valley High School. I'd been here before, but this time it was to report for the first day of a new job. Eventually finding the office in an old domestic science room on the ground floor, I spent a dismal day sitting around being briefed on the tasks ahead – to research and write a series of booklets of educational and community interest for this MSC funded scheme for the long-term unemployed. All the while, the smells of a building long expunged from memory wafted nauseatingly around me once more. Disinfectant, paint warming on iron radiators and the kitchen – always the kitchen – sited deep in the bowels of the structure.

Those first days passed slowly and idly, franked by organised, time-wasting, frustrating inertia. So we passed the time huddled in groups (there were around a dozen, all told, on the payroll), drawn by perceived similarities and talking around a variety of subjects by way of probing familiarity. One day we were joined by a self-conscious figure whose rheumy eyes bulged, squinted, peered and swivelled like blobs of cold jellied brawn from beneath deep purple hoods. Tall, gaunt and angular, he stooped as if born to do so and the overhanging Roman nose lent unnecessary age to an unshaven countenance. Clothed in an Oxfam ensemble of indeterminate vintage, his name was Dave Haslem, and Dave Haslem lived for music.

Soon, this was deemed a vital component of the working environment and indeed our physical and spiritual well-being. The acquisition of a cassette player from our bumptious, vacillating (though usually absent) supervisor, Brian, coincided with a move to the top floor of the building. If the music helped mesh us together, we now had a room with a view and a window to stare out of. And stare out of it we did – at the melancholy, fast-disappearing industrial landscape. Lower Broughton, Greengate and over in the distance, Strangeways. A fierce eclecticism was all that characterised the music we played; everything from Talking Heads to George Formby was heard against the wintry backdrop of those shortening days. And yet the thread of unity emerged which bound these musical predilections of frightening disparity – namely, that The Smiths were something to be proud of and treasured; something to be supported and cherished with every will and effort. Their tapes were played sparingly but to full effect, often in the quietening of a late afternoon when concentration on work tails off with the fading of light outside.

Thus it was, that after a month or so of such absorbed behaviour, the imminent release of a compilation of Radio One sessions and 'third tracks' generated its thyroidism of collective anticipation. As we gathered for work that cold, crisp Monday morning it was decided that if the dilatory Brian should disappear at lunchtime and not return, then a trip into town was called for so that *Hatful of Hollow* might be aboard our record players that very evening on returning home. Brian was as good as his habit, and it was with excitement unbridled that we disembarked from a number 93 beside Virgin Records on Market Street – there to be greeted by the sight of queues composed of Manchester's working truants lining the checkouts clutching the pale blue sleeve to their breasts.

The remainder of the afternoon passed in a buzz, fuelled by that potent energy born of high spirits and mutual self-congratulation. Dave, I recall, argued keenly that we should dally ostentatiously around the streets and shops, galleries and department stores in order that our thin, foot-square orange carrier bags could be brandished to the world as if in some 1960s 'England Swings!' promotional film. But we contented ourselves with examining in detail the sleeve contents and photocopying a million times over the Paul Slattery inner sleeve group portrait. And then, at last, buses from the gates in Conniston Street bound for home and tea and turntables . . .

That album contained one moment which prompted my writing in the first instance. The purest, most pungent distillation of a record which epitomised my feelings of atavistic time and place. Enduringly, these eleven years later, it still does: 'This Night Has Opened My Eyes.'

Unhappy Birthday

STEPHANIE LEGENDRE of Neuville-Sur-Oise, France

This goes back to 1988 – in spring, I think. I was going to an exhibition on vintage cars in quite a 'posh' district of Paris called 'Jardins de Bagatelle'. I was on the bus listening to *Strangeways . . .* on my walkman, sharing it with my sister. The trip was so long and we were surrounded by rather square people. When 'Unhappy Birthday' started we exchanged intense glances filled with understanding. At this very moment I felt so proud to be listening to The Smiths for it meant being totally different from these people, and it struck me that all I could ever wish them was an 'unhappy birthday'. I felt almost like an outlaw, and I smiled – thinking that had those people known what was going through our minds and into our ears they would certainly have sent us to such a place as Strangeways.

TON DE VRIES of Rotterdam, Holland

Around Christmas '94, I was advertising in the Dutch press for Smiths vinyl to boost my collection. Before long, and without payment, I received a most unexpected parcel from a girl: it contained a gatefold edition of *The Queen is Dead* and a short letter. Freely translated, this read:

I saw your request for Smiths vinyl and I give you this album with the greatest pleasure. Someone gave it to me for my birthday years ago and it was the worst birthday gift I ever got. I played it once and hated it – the 'singer' can't sing, the music is tedious and the lyrics are one big cliché. How can anyone like this shit? Apparently you do, so here it is – have fun with it.

Can you believe that? I sent her flowers in return. Fair trade for both of us, I guess.

Unloveable

MILLIE RUST of Hammersmith, London

First heard on a number 211 bus travelling to work experience interview. Seems pretty pertinent, in an economic way . . .

TON DE VRIES of Rotterdam, Holland

I teach statistics to freshmen and most of them have no interest in alternative music. So I was taken aback (and really pleased) when one of the students appeared to be a real Smiths fan. He was fifteen minutes late and wore a sad look on his face as he entered the lecture room. He was dressed entirely in black, which was unusual as he normally wore other clothes. I asked him during the break whether a funeral or something had made him late that day. He replied, 'I wear black on the outside . . .' and before he could finish I completed the line . . . 'because black is how you feel on the inside?' He looked at me with surprise. I was no longer a teacher but a fellow Smithsonian. Some weeks later, I was due to take the class for linear regression and followed his lead, as seemed entirely appropriate.

MELINDA HSU of Fresno, USA

Somehow and inexplicably, this song is a perfect fusion of emotion, words, melody, harmonies and instruments. Of course,

Morrissey's lyrics and voice are incredibly emotional and touching. How odd it is that someone who sings about insecurity and loneliness can seem so attractive. The song is a complex blend of true emotion and compelling contradiction. It's still a personal anthem even though I'm no longer a teenager all garbed in black inside and out. I can even be quite sociable and charming when I want to be these days, but there is always a sad, pitiful ghost in me who sings this song to herself.

Vicar In A Tutu

KEITH WRIGHT of County Armagh, N. Ireland

Coming from Ulster, having religion bombarded at you day and night, it's pretty difficult to imagine the concept of a 'vicar in a tutu' cavorting around and sliding down bannisters. Only The Smiths could have got away with such a song. Ian Paisley and his ilk would have Morrissey whipped for writing such irreverent drivel and if you think that's an exaggeration then try living over here!

DAVIDE FERRANTO of Vicenza, Italy

In compiling my Smiths top ten for you, I borrowed heavily from *The Queen is Dead*. Why? Because it was the first record to which I became addicted after years of Spandau Ballet and Dead Or Alive. The Smiths first caught my eye as a result of their brief appearances in the British singles chart during 1985 and 1986 and what little I could then understand of the music press in English.

Then one hot, sunny, wet Italian summer afternoon I saw a Smiths record for the first time in my life. It was this album and cost more or less all of the pocket money I had available. What if I was to spend all my precious cash and it turned out to be a shit record? After all, I hadn't heard a single note of most of the songs on that album. But I bought it, of course, otherwise I wouldn't be writing this today. Even without the benefit of a listen, it seemed to embody everything I asked of an album; it was on a British indie label and featured Alain Delon and a gatefold sleeve. The lyrics, at this time, were too far beyond my slim grasp of English for me to make any sense of.

The B-side seemed the best place to start, since it commenced with the couple of singles I *had* previously heard and loved. The next track took a little time to grow on me and even longer to make any sense. I had already come to adore it at a time when all I could make out was that it told the story of a bizarre man wearing women's clothes.

PATRICK LOWE of Acton, West London

When you're fourteen, being the son of the local vicar is not much fun. When I was younger I'd been fat, picked on, called all the usual names and had only one friend, and he was the other oddball in my year. I, of course, blamed my father. Why did he have to be a vicar and wear dresses and open-toed sandals? By the time I reached puberty I was totally lacking in confidence, and hated my father and his stupid 'job'. But I'd lost weight by almost starving myself and had grown quite a bit (5'11") and although I was almost completely useless at football, I did manage to make it into the second team as goalkeeper. From there on, I got what I had wanted so badly – to be one of the lads. And I did all I could to be accepted. I'd nick the communion wine and incense and take them to parties my new-found 'mates' were having. I thought getting drunk and throwing up on a Saturday night was the ultimate in being 'cool'. My parents couldn't understand what was going on. I'd been a fair student, always got Bs and C+s on exams and reports. But now they were getting letters from school saying that I wasn't turning up, and when I did I wasn't doing anything but disrupting classes with my pathetic 'jokes'. My father tried to reason with me, and did all the usual things, from bribery (a new bike! Wowee!) to punishment (grounded, but did I stay in? Nah.).

Then one Saturday night, after the usual four pints of lager and a bag of chips, someone – I can't remember who – started asking about my dad; whether it was true he liked dressing up as a woman, wearing a tutu. I was slightly too pissed to understand what was going on, and felt anger burning up my face, turning me red, making me ashamed and confused. I ended up punching this guy and jumping on him. When the other guys pulled me off they tried to calm me down, saying it was joke. Hadn't I heard 'Vicar In A Tutu'? They played it to me and I pretended to laugh and understand what was going on. Later, at home with my own copy, listening to the song (and the album), I slowly began to realise that it wasn't my father's fault that I was the way I was. It was my own.

Well I Wonder

SANDRA BANFIELD of Maravick, Canada

This song has been my favourite for a long, long time. It used to make me cry (embarrassing, frankly!), but now makes me smile, I'm glad to say. One dark night, I was driving home, listening to *Meat is Murder*. As usual, this song had me reaching for the volume control – more, please! I sang along, oblivious to the world around me and, it transpired, the red light which loomed up ahead . . .

Needless to say, the other drivers involved were not impressed and would not have been taken with my explanation!

NICK WAISENFELD of Burton-On-Trent, Staffordshire

I didn't really get into The Smiths until after they'd split up. I'd always been impressed by the songs I'd stumbled across on the radio and in clubs, but it wasn't until Christmas '88 that I became what you'd call 'a fan'.

The chap I shared a house with had gone off for the festive holiday, leaving me alone with the cat, 24 cans of ale, a small bag of wacky baccy and the pile of Smiths records I'd hired from the public library. High time I checked out this much-lauded group.

Having always subscribed to the 'Bah, humbug!' school of

Christmas cheer, it was no trauma whatsoever to be spending this time alone. Quite the reverse – I had been handed a marvellous opportunity to explore The Smiths 'canon' at my leisure.

Donning the quilted maroon smoking jacket picked up for ten pence at a jumble sale some months earlier, I reclined gracefully on the sofa like some late nineteenth-century aesthete. This, I considered, lent a suitably Wildean flavour to the proceedings and in any event, only Tiddles was around to witness my undoubted prattishness. Before long, I found myself transfixed by the melancholy beauty of tracks like 'Asleep' and 'This Night Has Opened My Eyes'.

The song which established itself as a particular favourite, however, was 'Well I Wonder'. The combination of Andy Rourke's sombre bassline with Morrissey's almost painfully introverted performance simply blew me away. Why is it that such desperately sad music can be hugely uplifting? Quoth the great man on some other pressing philosophical concern, 'I dunno'.

Anyway, that's about it. Christmas '88 will forever remain the Christmas Tiddles and myself became acquainted with the Mancunian Miserablists. It was one of the best ever, for both of us.

STUART MONTEITH of Lisburn, County Antrim

So many times I've felt this way over certain people ... I still see this girl around who I used to know years ago; she never fails to come to mind when I hear this song. She fancied me back then, but I didn't want to know. Now she's gorgeous and I wonder if she notices me at all.

The whole of *Meat is Murder* evokes my schooldays, and the many people from that era who've subsequently moved on and fallen out of touch – especially Julian and Carol. Also, the penfriends with whom I got in contact through a London-based fanzine: Amy, Stuart and Christine.

NEIL ASHMORE of Stockport, Cheshire

Poland – April '89, sitting in a Warsaw taxi headed for the railway station, staring at this strange city and mulling over that hoary old chestnut called life. The opening bars of this song comes over the driver's radio and as the grey rain recedes, I feel oddly inspired. Strange, eh?

RICHARD BRETT of Cheltenham, Gloucestershire

This song evokes an everyday scene and an insignificant few minutes from 1985. The day in question was cold and wet and I was part of a group of twenty of so bedraggled creatures loafing outside a dirty green 'terrapin-hut' in the Media Studies block of Bunswick Campus, Gloucester. It was our first day; the rain was persistent and the door locked. One hulking bruiser had tried unsuccessfully to force it, but he now leant against the wall nursing his shoulder and damaged pride. Nobody spoke much.

Then, through the storm, a latecomer. The bloke's name I forget, but I can still see his approach in the distance, ambling slowly through the puddles. He had a shock of blond hair and wore black jeans and a dark green morning jacket complete with tails. He joined the silent group, slouching against a wall, and as we quietly drowned, I remember wishing I was miles away.

JENNY GREEN of Sheffield, Yorkshire

Really, my story brings to mind *two* songs, both from *Meat is Murder*, but I should like it to be filed under 'Well I Wonder' in honour of a friendly (if conscientious!) policeman.

In May '89, I drove up from London to Doncaster for my sister Paula's 21st birthday party. The visit had to be a flying one, since the do was being held on a Wednesday night and I was due in the exam hall at two o'clock the following afternoon for the first of my university finals. The plan was to make my excuses around midnight, and with the benefit of a deserted M1, be back in my Cricklewood digs by 4 a.m. for what would amount to a normal, if slightly belated, night's sleep. After all, they *do* say that you don't learn any more the night before, so I was able to persuade myself that the trip wasn't as harebrained as my friends seemed to think.

The drive north was a joy in the big car I'd borrowed for the occasion and my efforts were amply repaid by a really fun night, albeit one fuelled by nothing more potent than apple spritzers. At midnight, I began my goodbyes to the assembled revellers and, grabbing a tape of *Meat is Murder* for the drive, pulled off sometime around half past. So far so good. My satisfaction continued to grow with the sound of The Smiths and the empty expanses of the southbound carriageway. Save for the inevitable freight trucks, the motorway resembled my own private racetrack. Oh, the joys of motoring! The needle scarcely wavered from 95 mph as I began to wonder if half an hour might not be trimmable from the journey time. End of tape – 'The Headmaster Ritual' once more . . . I would have listened all night, had not the blue flashing light loomed in my rear view. Shit.

Leaning on the sill, he seemed friendly enough; around 50 with a nice kind face. Definitely more Jack Warner than Robocop. His manner suggested a kind of, 'Actually, I don't blame you, but unfortunately I've *got* to do this' kind of attitude. We began to do the details. I was only semi-aware that the tape was still playing away, although I think I had turned the volume down somewhat. My benign captor was scribbling furiously on one of those 'rainbow' pads with more colours than Joseph's coat. Then an astonishing thing happened: without raising his eyes, he recited a line along with Morrissey. And not just any old line. 'He killed a policeman when he was thirteen, and somehow that really impressed me – it's written all over my face.' He then looked up and smiled, seeing no doubt, the mixture of bewilderment and shock on my face. 'If I've heard this bloody record once, I've heard it a thousand times. Daughter your age – she's nuts about The Smiths.' I really didn't know what to say, but being booked by this man was beginning to feel like an honour. Incredibly, there was more to come. 'Actually, there's a song later on which I like a lot – I think it's called "Well I Wonder", would that be right?' I confirmed that this was indeed correct and offered to fast-forward the tape if he wished. The whole episode was now assuming a kind of surreal quality, but of course he declined. I suppose he could listen anytime back home.

Interrogation over, my journey was completed at a sedate 68 mph and, after sleeping like a log, the exam was negotiated with scarcely a hiccough. Well, I *did* wonder if perhaps my ticket might get lost *en route*, such had been the relaxed atmosphere on the hard shoulder that night. But no – it arrived, right on cue within the month. For evermore, the line 'Do you see me when we pass' will conjure a mental picture of a police car sitting in darkness on a motorway slip road.

What Difference Does It Make?

MAIRI CLARE CUSHLEY of Bothwell, near Glasgow

Another Monday morning and another spiritual hangover from another mad weekend in Glasgow's Sub Club. But this one is particularly raw-edged. I have an afternoon appointment with the University of Glasgow Law Faculty degree exam. Crumpled, head in hands, I sit at the kitchen table contemplating doom and half-listening to an 'All Time Classics' compilation tape. I know it's too late – way too late – to learn the relevant statutes and cases which might furnish even token stabs at possible right answers.

The time marches – positively zooms, in fact. And without being aware of its passage the hour of reckoning is upon me. I gather up my pencil case and a few notes and prepare to make for the fray. Crossing the room, the opening bars of 'What Difference Does It Make?' burst from the tape player and echo round the room. I know the words so well . . . better by far than the legal litany I shall soon be asked to recite and regurgitate.

Outside, the west end basks in glorious sunshine and as my leaden feet cross Byres Road on to University Avenue the words reverberating inside my head are not those of my lecturer, but those of Steven Patrick Morrissey.

The exam hall, my place of execution, hoves into view alongside Kelvingrove Park. I gather both in my sights, looking at one and then the other, and at that the weirdest thing happens.

My legs just keep going; and with the pace, so does my heart quicken with release and elation.

And stopping eventually beside the dry and littered fountain, my head reels.

And the difference made was none.

RUSS C. S. THOMAS of Ferndale, South Wales

I've never understood the band's dislike of the single mix of this song. Every time I hear it I'm back in the youth club having insults (and occasional pasties), thrown at me for having the highest quiff there. Children can be so spiteful.

FIONA of Stoke-On-Trent, Staffordshire

Hearing the intoxicating intro to this song never fails to have a rather debilitating effect on me. It matters little what I am doing at the time; I am rendered entirely useless, awash on a wave of nostalgia. Back I go to the sweat-laden, condensation-filled hall that is Hull University student union. Morrissey towers above me – never before and never again have I made such an effort to be right at the front. Battered and bruised ribs bore testimony to this, but for that one night all that mattered was being right up there. 1984. Sweet sixteen, and as my greedy fingers grabbed and plucked the air, that demi-god casually tossed luridly coloured gladioli to the heaving throng. My efforts were rewarded with a limp piece of stem which had seemingly been passed through a mangle, but I cherished it none the less. Having had the breath squeezed from my body and been cracked on the head countless times, I finished the concert sitting on my own at the back, clutching my drooping prize and strangely content.

JO COOPER of Hampstead, London

I travelled to Reading in February '84 for one of the dates of The Smiths tour. 'What Difference Does It Make?' had just been released and things were really taking off. Aged just fifteen, I was yet to acquire the streetwisdom which might have enabled me to realise that Reading wasn't actually at the ends of the earth! The big adventure, 40 miles west of London . . . I should also have been at school.

My friend Emma, at eighteen, was cast in the role of 'grownup' and would handle any awkward situations which might arise. We had seen the band several times before in London, and having been fortunate (and forward!) enough to have met them, had been promised a place on the guest list at Reading. By way of a thank you, we arrived bearing gifts.

The main present, a teddy bear, was a feat of creative artistry and improvisation. We bought the pot-bellied bear from a shop on the King's Road, Chelsea and made straight for Emma's flat. Before long he was transformed into a Johnny Marr 'bear-a-like' thanks to Emma's talents as an infant teacher. 'Teddy-Marr' as we christened him, sported Ray-Ban glasses (made from black tights material), a red and gold cardboard Gretsch guitar and the obligatory hoop earring fashioned from wire and gold paper. *Blue Peter* eat your heart out!

We presented Johnny with Teddy-Marr at the soundcheck where our place on the guest list was confirmed. He enjoyed his fifteen minutes of fame sitting atop Johnny's amp throughout the gig. Incidentally, I recall Johnny sulking for a bit after someone threw a glass of water over him – he said his first fear was of possible electrocution, his second was that his hair might've been messed up.

Afterwards, we chatted to the band backstage and were offered a lift back to our B&B in their blue Transit van. Phil Powell (guitar-roadie extraordinaire) drove, with Johnny in the passenger seat while Emma and I sat in the back with Mike, Andy and Morrissey. We were on such a happy high, knowing that in a few days' time we'd be doing it all over again!

I sometimes wonder whatever became of Teddy-Marr. Doubtless he's living pretty quietly now, burned out by the excesses of a rock 'n' roll lifestyle!

STUART MONTEITH of Lisburn, County Antrim

The great outdoors! This track recalls a kind of adventure weekend I spent in County Down with a couple of school-friends and some others from around Belfast. I would play this all the time there. I really fancied one of the girls on the trip who came from a Belfast school. Afterwards, I requested the song on a local radio station and dedicated it to her and even sent her a copy of *The Queen is Dead*. Nothing ever came of it. Obviously, she wasn't too fussed on me, but I know that at that time, I'd definitely have leapt in front of a flying bullet for her . . .

RICK WESTLAKE of Lincoln

It's well documented that different civilisations and cultures have employed unusual units of currency; salt, teeth and hides all spring to mind, while in the here and now, half an ounce of loose shag cuts plenty of mustard in Wormwood Scrubs. For me and my gang of thirteen-year-old desperados, the planet held no more precious commodity than little white spheres, 1.62″ in diameter. Golf balls.

Mine is a story of greed and obsession: *The Treasure of Sierra Madre* played out under suburban skies with golf balls in place of gold. For we dreamt of golf balls, night and day. At school, in history class, I recall learning of some Aztec king whose ransom was set at enough gold to fill his prison cell to head height. The details are somewhat hazy, so absorbed was I in fantasising of a classroom half-filled with brand new Dunlop 65s. In maths, I calculated that around 1,600,000 would be required to achieve this, and trembled just a little at the thought. Golf balls, you see, could be turned into hard cash (between 10 and 30 pence depending on condition) and that cash into cigarettes and football admission, and no greater worldly wealth did we crave.

The means of procurement was, at once, time-consuming, laborious and madly exciting, since stalking the rough and copses of the local golf club carried no little risk. The club itself was extremely posh and notoriously conservative – its members disapproved strongly of grubby invaders, especially when they came on pilfering forays. And during the summer in question, the heat was really on; several of our number had been caught and held and cautioned by the police for trespassing. Thin times came – our hauls diminished most alarmingly and the ten-packs of Black Cat began to dry up. Our missions came to resemble military operations, with hides and camouflage and dawn raids through still dewy undergrowth. But the enemy was still in the ascendency – something had to be done to break the mould. Eventually, desperation begat The Grand Scheme . . .

Between the third and fourth fairways nestled a small pond, roughly circular and perhaps 30 yards across. Covered in thick weed and surface scum, in hot weather it bubbled and broiled like witches' brew and stank of natural gas. But our greedy nostrils also twitched at the scent of untold riches. Once, during a dry spell, its shallows had receded sufficiently to expose several dozen gleaming white pearls around the perimeter – a tantalising taster of what the murky depths might hold. We could either fashion a raft or pray for a cosmic explosion to throw the earth and sun into closer proximity.

Three railway sleepers were lashed together with an oil drum at either end. This was no lightweight racing clipper – it must have weighed more than a small car and took eight staggering schoolboys to carry it on to the course under dusk's gathering gloom. I was to pilot the vessel, and had been armed with a long-handled net plundered from someone's garden shed. The idea was to 'trawl' a certain area before being towed to fresh fishing grounds by means of the rope attached. Darkness had fallen by the time I climbed aboard and, propelled by a mighty shove, ploughed a yard-wide furrow of clear water through the surface gunge. This soup-like consistency, combined with primitive streamlining, allowed me to travel no further than two sleeper-lengths from shore. Despite this, I was now in a position to trawl virgin lakebed. Things were going swimmingly.

I shall never, ever forget that first tentative pass with the net. Up it came, heavy with mud and silt and slimy weed . . . and four balls. All told, we took around 120 from the deep that night – some fifteen apiece by the time the booty was divided amid the whoops of victory.

The Smiths? Oh yes, the point of the story. The next day, after resetting the spoils, I purchased a *twenty* pack of Black Cat. And a record. I suppose it should've been 'Straight Down The Middle' by Bing Crosby, but it wasn't. Instead I plumped for a seven-inch single whose blue-washed sleeve photograph appealed in some strange way. It featured a smiling man holding a glass of milk and sporting clothes which wouldn't have looked out of place on the fairways. That man was Morrissey, the band was The Smiths and very soon, golf balls ceased to be the central focus of my life.

COULTER of Portland, Maine, USA

I think my story starts in 1984, when I was thirteen years old. As a bespectacled, gawky adolescent, I wasn't quite part of the schoolyard societies which circled around me. My childhood had been filled with the pop idols of nearly 30 years earlier: Eddie Cochrane, Buddy Holly, Ricky Nelson and of course Elvis. Perhaps this, more than anything else, set me apart from my peers whose musical sights were trained firmly on the charts and didn't come complete with a rear-view mirror. Precious as my Brylcreemed heroes were, I was desperately keen to find someone to speak to me in the present tense – someone to relate to as a living, breathing person.

My search ended thanks to a nasty habit – snooping through my elder brother's record collection. It was there that I stumbled across a sampler tape from Sire Records. Aztec Camera, Scritti Politti, China Crisis . . . and then The Smiths. The song was this one and in retrospect it was to make all the difference in the world. Passion and poetry accompanied by an entrancing guitar riff. The same afternoon I went to the record store and bought the album – my first Smiths record.

Its songs and words became my everyday ammunition as I trudged through the next few years – to be used against those who mocked my hair, my clothes and my flowers. And defend them I did, with a zeal which would be recognisable only to those who've entered that faraway world. Was this unhealthy? Very possibly, but we all know dozens of people who could similarly defend these actions, these obsessions.

Just how do you explain to someone who listens to White-snake what The Smiths are all about? It's like talking in French to someone who only speaks Russian. Well, I survived it all . . . barely. I bought every album, every single, every T-shirt, every button, every magazine and fanzine – you name it. But the cloak of imagery merely hinted at what was beneath: what I saw in The Smiths (and in Morrissey to this day) was the perfect human representation of the way life should be lived in the imperfect world we find ourselves stuck with. Everything seemed just right in every way, and the fact that I faced condemnation from others for simply wearing a T-shirt was validation of the fact that I was right. That The Smiths were right.

It took several years to apply rationality to that which filled my adolescence. *Ordinary Boys* represented the (long-awaited) juncture at which I realised it was finally within my grasp to express what was troubling about the world and, most especially, what was so comforting about The Smiths. The book proved a catharsis for me. In writing it, I was able to use my own voice and my own words to articulate the importance of those vinyl grooves. I still listen to the songs most days. Now, I can sing my own words.

MARTIN COOPER of Glasgow, G2

Fourteen years old and in the town centre on a Friday night. The ornamental fountain had been turned into a luxurious bubble bath once again – some prankster with the washing-up liquid . . .

The Smiths had just played a local venue, although I'd never heard of them. A well-respected friend, who always knew the know before I did, turned up with flowers in his back pocket. We nicked some from a verge and did likewise, dancing around and acting the fool. I hadn't a clue what it was all about but we were having fun so what difference did it make?

NORMAN CUMMINS of Govan, Glasgow

Sitting watching the football of a Saturday lunchtime. No suicides in this one – except when Jimmy Hill was on!

KHRIS TIMMONS of Greenock, Renfrewshire

I was fourteen or fifteen and it was the occasion of a second year school disco. The hall was dark, smoky and the threat of violence hung heavy in the air due to the presence of a number of casuals from a neighbouring school. Midway through the night this song was played and it was quite unlike anything I'd ever before heard; the whole guitar sound, playground voices and that voice which was so detached yet resonant.

What She Said

CLIVE of Kingston, Surrey

It was one of those terminally boring Christmases with the extended family. I was about 21 and had recently acquired *Rank*. Politeness and protocol demanded that I participate in the endless succession of weary parlour games for which the Yuletide is notorious.

We played one which involved passing round slips of paper and writing down two names, a place, two sayings and a conclusion to the format of: (NAME) met (NAME) at (PLACE). He said (SAYING), she said (SAYING). The result was (OUTCOME) and the world said (CONCLUSION).

Anyway, when I came to fill in what 'she said', I plugged the blank with the rather lengthy, 'I smoke because I'm hoping for an early death and I need to cling to something.'

It fell to mother to read out my contribution, which she did with humorous, theatrical panache. Father told me not to be so stupid, and my aunt burst out laughing and a stony silence descended upon the rest. Interestingly, if predictably, no one expressed anything remotely resembling compassion.

I knew they wouldn't, but enjoyed the satisfaction which proof brought. After all, these were simply not the sort of people I wanted to understand.

EDD TRAVERS of Kirkintilloch, Nr Glasgow

I'm often branded a 'weirdo' because I like The Smiths, have a quiff and loathe football. Most times, I just let it slide, but when I get really pissed off I tend to play this angry song as a means of letting off steam. The central theme, of fighting for mere acceptance in this world, seems to preclude the possibility of anything more ambitious than that. For me, it lambasts the sickening mundanity of society and the shallow premium it places on 'normality'. In other words, why must life seem, so often, to be a crass celebration of braindead 'Betty's and shell-suited plastic 'hard-men'? The Smiths are my salvation from the tacky, artificial, bland, boring town in which I live.

SUZANNE FIRTH of Eastleigh, Hampshire

It all reminds me of sitting around a gorgeous oak table in summer during Mrs Moody's maths class. Three pubescent girls gorging themselves silly on a mammoth Milky Bar. Me hardly eating at all, but getting this Monday afternoon fix of sugar and Linnet's sex life. It was all so tawdry and council-housey, her rampant unprotected flings with 25-year-old plumbers from The Unity Club.

I wondered if that was all we had to look forward to for the foreseeable future – weekly rantings and rushing to the toilet to await the blood. Elaine and I were too cynical or too optimistic or perhaps too closeted to really believe that our fourteen-year-old lives wouldn't brighten considerably. Meantime, we succumbed to the sugar.

Elaine was fat but wise enough to give as good as she got. She was an avid hoarder of secrets and snippets and half-facts, told in confidence but told none the less. I was sure she'd change the world; this beautiful, self-accepting Mama Cass figurine, serene and calm – an Earth Mother who told us to sit cross-legged and feel the planet breathe around us. Linnet tried this, in-between plumbers. Time passed slowly – people and events assuming terrific importance. One day Elaine passed out on the stairs to the typing rooms, to be rescued by her brother – Mephistopheles – who slept open-eyed like a crocodile. I always expected her maths book to be covered in chicken shit because she said the hens shared their house.

I started smoking that year and scabbed fags outside the school gates. Mrs Moody's attempts to quell rebellion merely fuelled the fire and in any event, what chance did she have as pumping testosterone created obscene hand puppets on her projector screen? Early death *did* seem attractive – tragically, perhaps, in the company of *Das Kapital* or Sylvia Plath. Or serenely, floating off with Ophelia. But if I didn't starve or smoke myself to death, I knew the only real option was suffocation underneath a bargain Argos beanbag. And I could never have done that to my parents.

William, It Was Really Nothing

IAIN KEY of Cheadle, Cheshire

I went to see Suzanne Vega at the Manchester Apollo in November '86. She said she'd been playing this acoustically on the tour bus and hoped Morrissey was in the audience because she admired him greatly and loved The Smiths. Was he?

MARK ZORRO of Hackney, London

My brother is going out with a stingy girl who's never dreamt of anyone or anything. My brother doesn't like The Smiths. So I have to like them on his behalf.

DAVID BARBER of Rochdale, Lancashire

Ruth was a new girl at my high school in Rochdale in 1984 – I think she'd been expelled from her old one in Middleton. She was looked down upon by most of her classmates; she seemed a bit thick, a bit tartish and tacky, even scruffy; just one of those unpopular kids at school who were seen as not having a clue with regard to 'what was cool'. She left our school pretty soon after she came. The next time I saw her was in a town centre pub, probably a year or two later, doing a spot of under age drinking – she was quite unrecognisable. Gone was the crappy 'new romantic' inspired hair with homemade peroxide fringe, the cheap pencil skirt, scuffed heels and plasters. She now wore a Smiths T-shirt, the obligatory Doc Martens and a lot of black – eighties student-style. She talked incessantly about The Smiths, a band vaguely familiar to me: hadn't they done a song called 'William . . .' something or other . . . ? We ended up singing it together, both pissed – me knowing hardly any of the lyrics or the tune – and dressed like a complete arse in pegged trousers and awful shirt, and being more inclined to select a Duran Duran tune from the jukebox. In retrospect, it seems she had much more of a clue than myself or any other of her ex-classmates.

I began to discover The Smiths much later – around 1988. I remember working in a factory and singing out loud to the radio which was playing 'William' – '. . . How could you stay, with a fat girl who'd say . . .' – and at the same time catching the eye of my workmate who was, for want of a better description . . . a fat girl.

Both trivial incidents perhaps, but they invariably come to mind when I play the song and always play a part in the imagery it produces.

Wonderful Woman

RUSS C. S. THOMAS of Ferndale, South Wales

This is a song I dusted off and rediscovered recently after receiving a letter from a girl I'd not heard from for years. We met when I worked in Cardiff's HMV store back in 1985–6. She'd seen me parading around in a collection of Smiths T-shirts and began bringing flowers to the shop for me. On the first occasion she did this, I was playing 'Wonderful Woman' and as Morrissey cried 'I'm starved of love . . .' I thanked her with an almost perfect blush.

Her letter began, 'Are you still starving . . . ?' and I played the track again, fell in love again and didn't reply.

JOHN of Halifax, West Yorkshire

Alcoholic afternoons sitting on the window-sill in her bedroom, listening to The Smiths and Prefab Sprout, making plans and knowing we had something that would last for ever. Decorating her room together, me playing guitar, us fighting and her crying and then her laughing again. Staying all night at parties and walking across the common back to her house at dawn. That summer, those school holidays, seemed to last forever. Just the opening notes to this record brings it all back so effortlessly.

The Smiths were an inextricable part of that time. So much

so that it's hard to believe we could have had what we had if they weren't around.

We split up a year later. The fighting had got worse and the laughing had stopped.

Work Is A Four Letter Word

NOBUAKI NOMURA of Tokyo, Japan

I know this is not a Smiths original, but a line in the song rang in my head constantly at the time of an important turning point in my life. This decision owed so much to The Smiths that I often look back and consider just how significant they were – for me at least! I'd studied your language mostly through movies and rock and of course spent much time translating the words of Morrissey's songs. Not easy sometimes! After a time I decided I wanted to become a freelance translator and left the job I then had (which *definitely* made work seem like a four letter word). Fortunately, contacting lots of record companies here I've been given the opportunity to translate excellent music including The Eurythmics and The Wedding Present, along with those I don't like so very much like AOR. The record companies and publishers in my country always seem to find the best translators for The Smiths and Morrissey songs and books. Hopefully some day I'll be one of them. So to the song, 'Work Is A Four Letter Word'. It says: 'So change your life, there is so much I know that you can do . . .' That song (one of the first I translated) and my love of The Smiths *did* change my life.

HOLLY CAMERON of London, N19

This record springs to mind every time I go back home to my mum's in Blackburn and look out of her bedroom window where I can see the house where my ex-boyfriend now lives with his wife.

We started going out with each other when we were fourteen. We met at school; I was quiet, shy and regarded as slightly odd because I liked The Smiths; he was loud, confident and good-looking. Consequently, it came as a bit of a surprise to everyone, myself included, when it was me he chose to adorn with a love-bite one night at a party.

I suppose I should have known that a relationship with a Queen fan was doomed to failure but for some reason it lasted almost two years. Acquiring a taste for cider probably helped but despite our differences we got on well and yes, I did eventually convert him to my way of thinking about The Smiths (without having to reciprocate and buy everything Freddie Mercury had ever committed to vinyl).

It was when we reached the grand old age of sixteen and he began work that things started to go wrong. He left school to get a job in the bank, and became straighter each day, while I went to art college and made new friends, sheepishly admitting that my boyfriend was 'the one behind the counter at Barclays with the sensible haircut'. It was not to last and the time had come to tell him.

He wasn't surprised. By this time we could barely stand the sight of each other. Now there was only one thing left to sort out. We had tickets for The Smiths and we certainly weren't going to go together. Finally, after endless arguments, I came to the gloomy conclusion that he could have them if it meant I could walk away and never have to speak to him again.

I never did speak to him again so I never did find out what the gig was like, and eight years on, I still can't quite believe that I backed down and let him go instead of me. But I always smile to myself when I see him now, settled down like I always knew he would be, cutting the lawn or cleaning his car, his wife doing the ironing in the bedroom.

You've Got Everything Now

ANNA LLOYD of Chudleigh, Devon

For me, 'You've Got Everything Now' serves as a poignant epilogue to all the teenage angst and doleful tears shed throughout the difficult years of adolescence. But as once more my tenuous façade of happiness crumbles, I firmly close the bedroom door and switch the needle to the second track on the debut album. Drowning into a state of mild subconsciousness, I'm transfixed by the voice of a man who has so obviously felt the same way I do. An anthem for all the anguish and oppression I feel to this day, the song voices a bitter undertone of resentment which sometimes feels just too close to home. Could this be *my* feeling of envy which occasionally surfaces towards friends who appear to have emerged unscathed and triumphant on the other side of adolescence? They've got everything now . . .

ADAM of Norwich, Norfolk

It's a horrific cliché but this song does evoke powerful memories. Sometimes I feel that the only method I have of remembering my life so far is to use songs, as points on a map, to pin-point specific instances. The Smiths were always going to be a band which would appeal to me, into which I would dive headlong, immerse myself in and surround myself with.

All Men Have Secrets

The first LP was, and is (predictably) my favourite by far, and 'You've Got Everything Now' stands out as encapsulating that period in my life. The majority of my schooldays were spent in horrific boarding schools. These years were hell and my only escape was through music. The words of this song seemed to fit all the angles of my situation. 'You've Got Everything Now' was the person I was looking for, the person I wanted to be, the happiness I could almost have, tantalisingly close yet never quite reachable. They had everything and I didn't. They were the bullies, they were the feared ones, they were the ones with the girls. If I could only be seen with them ('in the back of the car'), if I could only be like them, then maybe everything would change.

When I reached sixteen I started to grow amazingly tall (amazing compared to my previously short, fat stature) and I grasped this as a chance to change my character – into a loud, obnoxious extrovert. But for all this I was niggled by horrendous self-doubt and a thin skin. It was these feelings that tapped so readily into this song. 'I was right and you were wrong' summed up my perpetual arrogance, which didn't even fool me, and 'back at the old grey school' reminded me of those nightmarish prep-school years which really had an awful lot to answer for.

I was taken by the music, but without doubt the words were what helped. Helped heal the wounds (now closed), and let me talk to another who at some time had suffered similar anomie.

You Just Haven't Earned It Yet, Baby

MARTIN COOPER of Glasgow

They say the greatest rock 'n' roll bands are those which older generations find most repugnant. Be that as it may, The Smiths were of course universally loathed by baby-boomers upon whom the comic tragedy of it all was entirely lost. Almost without exception, they failed to spot the bloom in the gloom. Well, at least that's the theory. One I knew exhibited greater insight and humour than most by fitting her own lyric to this song. 'You've just had your furniture painted, you've just had your furniture done . . .' And DIY was never the same again!

BRIDGET LEONARD of London, NW5

Maria was beautiful. She had long, black hair, high, sharp cheekbones and the finest skin you've ever seen; it shone like old china. We were both fifteen and at the same boarding school. I'd have done anything for her. So I did. At first it was simply fetching sweets from the tuck shop, books from the library or helping her with classwork. Then it became different, real jobs – like washing her clothes, cleaning her shoes and making her bed. I didn't mind. I'd have done it for a smile, and that's what I got, mostly. Then, one spring term she asked me for money. So I gave her all I had, but it wasn't enough. So I stole it. The first time was so terrifying – fumbling in blazer pockets while girls were in the shower – that when she asked me to steal for her again, I had to refuse. She said she hated me, and wouldn't talk to me anymore. For a week I was desperately lonely: I cried myself to sleep every night gazing across the dorm at Maria, who always turned her back to me. The only comfort I had was a small transistor radio that I kept under my bedcovers, tuned permanently to John Peel. It was the time when he was playing a lot of Smiths stuff, and I found the music strange, but somehow comforting in the warm, orange glow of my bed.

Maria made friends with Pauline, who began to do all the things I used to for Maria. But she refused to steal for her. So Maria returned to me.

What did I want?

My heart stopped. I felt afraid but elated. Dare I? 'Be my special friend.'

At school, special friends slept together. Their soft moans and panting could be heard just after lights out. I didn't know what they were doing, but knew that I wanted to find out.

Maria's smile twisted slightly. 'And what makes you think that you could possibly do anything to deserve that?' she snorted. She turned and walked away. That night as I simpered in my adolescent immaturity, the radio played 'You Just Haven't Earned It Yet, Baby' and I was amazed. How did Morrissey know? However he knew then, he continued – and continues – to know now. And when I wonder why 'all the love that (I) long for eludes (me),' I let him tell me.

Discography

Hand In Glove/Handsome Devil
Rough Trade RT 132. Released May 1983.

This Charming Man/Jeane
Rough Trade RT 136. Released November 1983.

This Charming Man (Manchester)/This Charming Man (London)/Accept Yourself/Wonderful Woman
Rough Trade RT 136 12". Released November 1983.

This Charming Man (New York)/This Charming Man (instrumental)
(Now deleted but may be found in large stores.)
Rough Trade 136. Released December 1983.

What Difference Does It Make?/Back To The Old House
Rough Trade RT 146. Released January 1984.

What Difference Does It Make?/Back To The Old House/These Things Take Time
Rough Trade RT 146 12". Released February 1984.

Hand In Glove/I Don't Owe You Anything
(Sandie Shaw with The Smiths)
Rough Trade RT 130. Released April 1984.

All Men Have Secrets

Hand In Glove/I Don't Owe You Anything/Jeane
(Sandie Shaw with The Smiths)
Rough Trade RT 130 12″. Released April 1984.

Heaven Knows I'm Miserable Now/Suffer Little Children
Rough Trade RT 156. Released May 1984.

Heaven Knows I'm Miserable Now/Suffer Little Children/Girl Afraid
Rough Trade RT 156 12″. Released May 1984.

William, It Was Really Nothing/Please Please Please Let Me Get What I Want
Rough Trade RT 166. Released August 1984.

William, It Was Really Nothing/Please Please Please Let Me Get What I Want/How Soon Is Now?
Rough Trade RT 166 12″. Released August 1984.

How Soon is Now?/Well I Wonder
Rough Trade RT 176. Released February 1985.

How Soon Is Now?/Well I Wonder/Oscillate Wildly
Rough Trade RT 176 12″. Released February 1985.

Shakespeare's Sister/What She Said
Rough Trade RT 181. Released March 1985.

Shakespeare's Sister/What She Said/Stretch Out And Wait
Rough Trade RT 181 12″. Released March 1985.

That Joke Isn't Funny Anymore/Meat Is Murder (live)
Rough Trade RT 186. Released July 1985.

That Joke Isn't Funny Anymore/Nowhere Fast (live)/Stretch Out And Wait (live)/Shakespeare's Sister (live)/Meat Is Murder (live)
Rough Trade RT 186 12″. Released July 1985.

The Boy With The Thorn In His Side/Asleep
Rough Trade RT 191. Released October 1985.

Big Mouth Strikes Again/Money Changes Everything
Rough Trade RT 192. Released May 1986.

Big Mouth Strikes Again/Money Changes Everything/Unloveable
Rough Trade RT 192 12". Released May 1986.

Panic/Vicar In A Tutu
Rough Trade RT 193. Released July 1986.

Panic/Vicar In A Tutu/The Draize Train
Rough Trade RTT 193 12". Released July 1986.

Ask/Cemetry Gates
Rough Trade RT 194. Released October 1986.

Ask/Cemetry Gates/Golden Lights
Rough Trade RTT 194 12". Released October 1986.

Ask/Cemetry Gates/Golden Lights
Rough Trade RTT 194c cassingle. Released October 1986.

Shoplifters Of The World Unite/Half A Person
Rough Trade RT 195. Released January 1987.

Shoplifters Of The World Unite/Half A Person/London
Rough Trade RTT 195 12". Released January 1987.

You Just Haven't Earned It Yet, Baby/Half A Person/London
(Mispress 12". January 1987.)

Sheila Take A Bow/Is It Really So Strange?
Rough Trade RT 196. Released April 1987.

Sheila Take A Bow/Is It Really So Strange?/Sweet And Tender Hooligan
Rough Trade RTT 196 12". Released April 1987.

Girlfriend In A Coma/I Keep Mine Hidden
Rough Trade RT 197. Released July 1987.

Girlfriend In A Coma/I Keep Mine Hidden/Work Is A Four Letter Word
Rough Trade RTT 197 12". Released July 1987.

I Started Something I Couldn't Finish/Pretty Girls Make Graves
Rough Trade RT 198. Released October 1987.

I Started Something I Couldn't Finish/Pretty Girls Make Graves/Some Girls Are Bigger Than Others
Rough Trade RTT 198 12". Released October 1987.

Last Night I Dreamt That Somebody Loved Me/Rusholme Ruffians
Rough Trade RT 200. Released December 1987.

Last Night I Dreamt That Somebody Loved Me/Rusholme Ruffians/Nowhere Fast
Rough Trade RTT 200 12". Released December 1987.

ALBUMS

THE SMITHS
Rough Trade ROUGH 61.
Released February 1984.
Reel Around The Fountain/You've Got Everything Now/Miserable Lie/Pretty Girls Make Graves/The Hand That Rocks The Cradle/Still Ill/Hand In Glove/What Difference Does It Make?/I Don't Owe You Anything/Suffer Little Children.

HATFUL OF HOLLOW
Rough Trade ROUGH 76.
Released November 1984.
William, It Was Really Nothing/What Difference Does It Make?/These Things Take Time/This Charming Man/How Soon Is Now?/Handsome Devil/Hand In Glove/Still Ill/Heaven Knows I'm Miserable Now/This Night Has Opened My Eyes/You've Got Everything Now/Accept Yourself/Girl Afraid/Back To The Old House/Reel Around The Fountain/Please Please Please Let Me Get What I Want.

MEAT IS MURDER
Rough Trade ROUGH 81.
Released February 1985.
The Headmaster Ritual/Rusholme Ruffians/I Want The One I Can't Have/What She Said/That Joke Isn't Funny Anymore/Nowhere Fast/Well I Wonder/Barbarism Begins At Home/Meat Is Murder.
(Also available as compact disc: Rough Trade ROUGH CD 81, released April 1985.)

THE QUEEN IS DEAD
Rough Trade ROUGH 96.
Released June 1986.
The Queen Is Dead/Frankly, Mr Shankly/I Know It's Over/Never Had No One Ever/Cemetry Gates/Big Mouth Strikes Again/The Boy With The Thorn In His Side/Vicar In A Tutu/There Is A Light That Never Goes Out/Some Girls Are Bigger Than Others.

THE WORLD WON'T LISTEN
Rough Trade ROUGH 101.
Released March 1987.
Panic/Ask/London/Big Mouth Strikes Again/Shakespeare's Sister/There Is A Light That Never Goes Out/Shoplifters Of The World Unite/The Boy With The Thorn In His Side/Asleep/Unloveable/

Half A Person/Stretch Out And Wait/That Joke Isn't Funny Anymore/Oscillate Wildly/You Just Haven't Earned It Yet, Baby/Rubber Ring.

LOUDER THAN BOMBS
Sire. 9 25568-1. (Double US Import.)
Released April 1987.
Is It Really So Strange?/Sheila Take A Bow/Shoplifters Of The World Unite/Sweet And Tender Hooligan/Half A Person/London/Panic/Girl Afraid/Shakespeare's Sister/William, It Was Really Nothing/You Just Haven't Earned It Yet, Baby/Heaven Knows I'm Miserable Now/Ask/Golden Lights/Oscillate Wildly/These Things Take Time/Rubber Ring/Back To The Old House/Hand In Glove/Stretch Out And Wait/Please Please Please Let Me Get What I Want/This Night Has Opened My Eyes/Unloveable/Asleep.

STRANGEWAYS HERE WE COME
Rough Trade ROUGH 106.
Released September 1987.
A Rush And A Push And The Land Is Ours/I Started Something I Couldn't Finish/Death Of A Disco Dancer/Girlfriend In A Coma/Stop Me If You Think You've Heard This One Before/Last Night I Dreamt That Somebody Loved Me/Unhappy Birthday/Paint A Vulgar Picture/Death At One's Elbow/I Won't Share You.